LONDON'S GREEN WALKS

20 Walks Around the City's Best Parks, Gardens & Waterways

by David Hampshire

CITY BOOKS

City Books • Bath • England

First published 2018

Copyright © Survival Books 2018
Cover design: Eoghan O'Brien
Cover photo: Thames Path, Richmond
Maps © Jim Watson

City Books, c/o Survival Books Limited
Office 169, 3 Edgar Buildings
George Street, Bath BA1 2FJ, United Kingdom
+44 (0)1305-266918
info@survivalbooks.net
www.survivalbooks.net and www.londons-secrets.com

British Library Cataloguing in Publication Data
A CIP record for this book is available
from the British Library

ISBN: 978-1-909282-82-7

Printed in China

Acknowledgements

The author would like to thank all the many people who helped with research and provided information for this book. Special thanks are due to Alex Browning for her invaluable research, Graeme & Louise Chesters and Richard Todd; Robbi Forrester Atilgan for editing; Peter Read for additional editing and proof-reading; Susan Griffith for final proof checking; John Marshall for DTP, photo selection and cover design; and Jim Watson for the lovely maps.

Last, but not least, a special thank you to the many photographers – the unsung heroes – whose beautiful images bring London to life.

ACCESS

All parks and gardens provide wheelchair access unless noted otherwise. Note, however, that this doesn't always apply to buildings within parks or WCs. Contact parks and gardens if you have specific requirements. The Disabled Go website (www. disabledgo.com) provides more in-depth access information for many destinations.

Author's Notes

Please note the following regarding the walks in this book.

♦ **Length & Duration:** The length of walks is approximate – shown to the nearest half or quarter mile – as is the time required to complete them, particularly if you make a lot of stops (coffee, lunch, museums, shopping, etc.). The average walking speed is around 3.1 mph but we have allowed for a much slower pace of 2 mph. (The idea isn't to get from the start to finish in as short a time as possible.) You can, of course, start a walk from either end and combine a number of walks to make a longer walk. Most walks are graded easy or moderate with relatively few hills or steps.

♦ **Opening Hours:** Most of the green spaces included in the walks are open seven days a week (opening hours are shown); times may differ for weekdays/weekends and in winter and summer. However, some private gardens are only open for limited hours on certain days or in certain months (as indicated). Almost all parks and gardens offer free access, unless otherwise indicated. The opening hours of many sights and museums (etc.) are listed. Bear in mind that these are liable to change. Where there's an entry fee, it's noted.

♦ **Transport:** All walks start and end at or near a tube or railway station. Most can also be reached by bus (routes aren't listed as there are simply too many to include them all) and sometimes by river ferry. The postcode of the starting point is shown should you wish to drive. However, you should bear in mind that the nearest car park or on-road parking may be some distance away, particularly in central London, and can be expensive.

♦ **Maps:** Note that maps aren't drawn to scale. Points of interest are numbered. An overall map of London is included on pages 8-9 showing the location of walks.

♦ **Food & Drink:** Recommended 'pit stops' have been included in all walks – shown in yellow in the map key and in the text. If you're planning to stop at one of the recommended places bear in mind that many only serve lunch between, say, noon and 2.30 or 3pm. Many pubs are also open in the mornings for coffee, etc. When not listed a pub/restaurant's opening times are the 'standard' times, e.g. noon-2.30pm and 6-11pm, although some are open all day and may also serve food all day (as do cafés). Telephone numbers are shown where bookings are advisable, otherwise booking isn't usually necessary or even possible. A price guide is included (£ = inexpensive, ££ = moderate); most recommended places fall into the inexpensive category.

♦ **Dogs:** Some parks and gardens don't permit dogs or they may need to be kept on a lead. Where applicable, this is noted.

Contents

Stag, Richmond Park

Introduction

Despite its reputation for noise and pollution, London is more verdant than any other world city of its size. Green spaces cover almost 40 per cent of Greater London, providing a profusion of places where you can walk, play, relax, exercise and commune with nature. The capital's green bounty ranges from magnificent royal parks and garden cemeteries, full of intrigue and history, to majestic ancient forests and barely tamed heathland; from elegant squares and formal country parks to enchanting 'secret' gardens.

The 20 walks in this book take in prominent destinations, such as Hyde and Regent's Park, but also many smaller and less familiar (but no less beautiful) parks and gardens, such as the New River Path and Ravenscourt Park, most of which cost nothing to explore. When you need a rest there's usually somewhere to sit down, thanks to Londoners' long tradition of donating benches in memory of departed loved ones.

With the exception of the royal parks – which owe their existence to the British monarchy's (and particularly Henry VIII's) passion for chasing deer – the majority of London's public parks were founded by the Victorians, from the 1840s onwards, as part of a range of measures to improve the living conditions of the working classes. London's living network of green lungs and waterways is still vital to the health and wellbeing of its inhabitants today. It also provides food and refuge for the city's flora and fauna, which – despite living alongside almost 9 million people – is extraordinary in its abundance, variety and scope.

Most walks are between two and five miles in length, with the average around 3½ miles. However, it's best to allow a half day for the shorter walks and as much as a full day for the longer walks – particularly if you plan to partake of the many excellent pubs, restaurants and cafés along the routes (for your author, a good lunch is a prerequisite of a good walk) – not to mention the many diversions along the way, such as museums, galleries and churches. Our aim was to take the 'scenic route', visiting as many interesting landmarks as possible, rather than simply getting from A to B.

Writing *London's Green Walks* has been a fascinating, edifying and enjoyable journey of discovery. We hope that you enjoy these walks as much as we did; all you need is a comfortable pair of shoes, a sense of adventure – and this book!

David Hampshire
January 2018

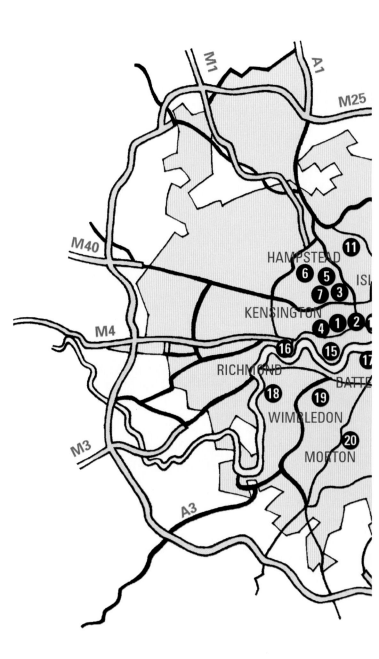

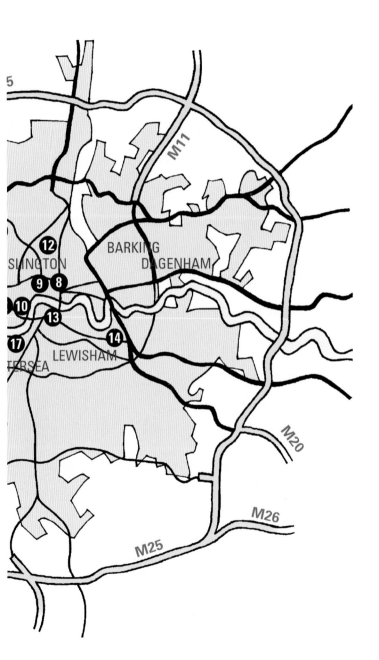

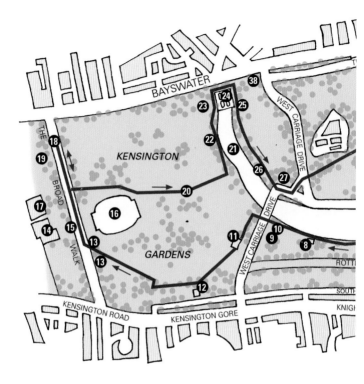

1 Rose Garden	**14** Kensington Palace
2 Boy & Dolphin Fountain	**15** Coalbrookdale Gates
3 Weeping Beech	**16** The Round Pond
4 Holocaust Memorial	**17** The Orangery
5 Serpentine Bar & Kitchen	**18** Diana, Princess of Wales Memorial
6 The Serpentine	**19** Elfin Oak
7 Queen Caroline Memorial	**20** Physical Energy Statue
8 The Lido	**21** The Long Water
9 Princess of Wales Fountain	**22** Peter Pan Statue
10 Isis Sculpture	**23** Two Bears Fountain
11 Serpentine Gallery	**24** Italian Gardens
12 Albert Memorial	**25** Jenner Statue
13 St Govor's Well & Tiffany Fountains	**26** Henry Moore Arch

● Places of Interest ○ Food & Drink

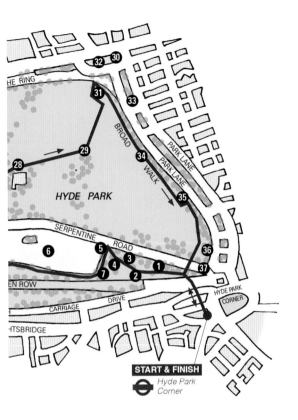

Hyde Park & Kensington Gardens

WALK 1

Distance: 5m (8km)
Terrain: easy, flat terrain
Duration: 2½ hours
Open: Hyde Park, 5-6am to midnight;
Kensington Gardens, 6am to dusk
Start/End: Hyde Park Corner tube
Postcode: SW1X 7LY

F or such a large and crowded city, London is unusually rich in parks, and among the largest and most rewarding are Hyde Park and Kensington Gardens – two of the city's eight ancient royal parks. Originally owned by the British monarchy and used for their private recreation (mostly hunting), with the increasing urbanisation of London in the 19th century, some royal parks were preserved as freely accessible open space and, with the introduction of the Crown Lands Act, 1851, they became public parks. Today, they are managed by the Royal Parks charity (www.royalparks.org.uk) and provide Londoners with a wealth of vast green playgrounds in and around the city, often aptly referred to as the city's green lungs.

Hyde Park is the largest of central London's royal parks, covering 350 acres (142ha). It was created in 1536 when Henry VIII seized land belonging to Westminster Abbey to use as a deer park (deer were hunted there until 1768) and was opened to the public in 1637 when it quickly became a popular destination, particularly for May Day parades. The Parliamentarians assumed control of the park for military use during the Civil War and Charles II enclosed it for the first time after the Restoration of the monarchy in 1660.

Kensington Gardens were formerly the grounds of Nottingham House, which became Kensington Palace when William III acquired it in 1689. Originally part of Hyde Park, the gardens (275 acres/111ha) have been a separate green space since 1728. They were first opened to the public in 1733, but only on Saturdays or Sundays, and there was a strict dress code that required visitors to wear wigs, feathers and (for the ladies) wide hooped skirts. The official boundary with Hyde Park is West Carriage Drive and the bridge that

Hyde Park & Kensington Gardens

Serpentine Bar & Kitchen

crosses the Serpentine (lake); the western section of the lake, the Long Water, lies within Kensington Gardens.

The eight royal parks – which include the largest green spaces in central London – cover a total area of almost 4,900 acres (2,000ha). In addition to the two parks featured in this walk, **Green Park and St James's Park (Walk 2), Regent's Park (Walk 3), Greenwich Park (Walk 14) and Richmond Park (Walk 18) also feature in this book.**

Start Walking…

Leaving Hyde Park Corner tube station, enter the park and take the path immediately on the left which leads to the lovely **Rose Garden** ❶. Look for a pair of low gates slightly to the right of the path. These take you towards two fountains: the Huntress (erected in 1899) on the left and the charming **Boy and Dolphin** ❷ on the right, featuring a pre-Raphaelite marble sculpture of a cherub and dolphin by Alexander Munro dating from 1862. Look carefully and you'll see that the water flows from the nostrils of the dolphin, not its mouth.

Opened in 1994, the spectacular Rose Garden features trellises and rose and herbaceous planting (it's at its best in early summer), creating rich seasonal flowerbeds and enticing aromas. Close by you'll find the **Weeping Beech** ❸ (on the right), also known as the Upside Down Tree

as its branches descend from the crown and look like roots. Continuing along the path you pass the Nannies' Lawn on your right and the **Holocaust Memorial** ❹ on your left, inscribed with the words: 'For these I weep. Streams of tears flow from my eyes because of the destruction of my people.'

At the end of the path you come to the **Serpentine Bar & Kitchen** ❺, which serves good seasonal food at reasonable prices in an attractive garden setting. Continue south along the eastern edge (head) of the **Serpentine** ❻ – an artificial lake created in 1730 for Queen Caroline (wife of King George II) from a string of natural ponds along the River Westbourne – which, along with the Long Water, divides Hyde Park from Kensington Gardens. Continue along the southern bank of the lake, passing the **Queen Caroline Memorial** ❼, an unprepossessing stone urn on a plinth overlooking the lake.

Follow the lake's edge and after a few minutes you arrive at Lutyens Drinking Fountain (there's another on the opposite side of the lake), named for one of Britain's finest 20th-century architects, Sir

Edwin Lutyens (1869-1944). It's located just before the **Lido** ⑧, home to Britain's oldest swimming club – and the venue for their Peter Pan Cup Christmas Day Race. Less hardy bathers should take a dip from May to September when the water is warmer – there's also a café and bar. Carry on along the edge of the lake, passing the **Diana, Princess of Wales Memorial Fountain** ⑨ on the left; designed by Kathryn Gustafson and opened in 2004, the fountain aims to reflect Diana's life, flowing from the highest point in two directions as it cascades,

swirls and bubbles before meeting in a calm pool at the bottom.

Straight ahead is the **Isis Sculpture** ⑩, a striking bronze by Simon Gudgeon, inspired by the Egyptian goddess of nature. Some 100m further on you come to West Carriage Drive. Cross over the road and take the path straight ahead, then turn left almost immediately and take the right-hand fork (away from the lake), which leads to the **Serpentine Gallery** ⑪ (see box).

From the gallery take the diagonal path in the southwest corner (behind the gallery), crossing over the Flower Walk to the magnificent **Albert Memorial** ⑫. Situated on the southern edge of Kensington Gardens – opposite the Royal Albert Hall – it commemorates Queen Victoria's adored husband who died of typhoid fever in 1861, aged just 42. This grand, high-Victorian Gothic extravaganza was

Hyde Park & Kensington Gardens

designed by Sir Gilbert Scott and unveiled in 1872. It incorporates a gilt-bronze statue of Albert and celebrates the achievements of the Victorian age and empire, with massive marble sculptures of the continents and a delicately carved frieze of painters, poets, sculptors, musicians and architects.

Continue along South Flower Walk and take the next path on your right and then the diagonal path to the left leading to Kensington Palace. Along the way you'll pass a bandstand (1931) on your right and, a little further on, the **St Govor's Well and Tiffany Drinking Fountains** **13** ; the former marks the site of an ancient spring and is named after a 6th-century hermit. At the junction of Mount Walk and the Broad Walk, turn right and almost immediately on your left is **Kensington Palace** **14** (see box). One of London's best-preserved palaces, it's where Queen Victoria was born (in 1819) and lived until her accession to the throne in 1837. The magnificent ornate wrought-iron

---

Kensington Palace

Kensington Palace has been a royal residence since 1689 – before Buckingham Palace was built – and has a fascinating historical and archaeological heritage. It was built in the early 17th century for the Earl of Nottingham and was purchased in 1689 by King William III and his wife Mary II, who wanted to escape from damp and dirty Whitehall Palace.

For many people it's inextricably linked with the late Diana, Princess of Wales, and the vast sea of floral tributes spreading out from the gates following her death in 1997. Fittingly, her son William and his wife Catherine (the Duke and Duchess of Cambridge) live there now. You can access the spectacular palace gardens free from Kensington Gardens without paying to visit the palace. See www.hrp.org.uk/kensington-palace for information.

Coalbrookdale Gates **15** were designed by Charles Crookes and made for the Great Exhibition in 1851. Opposite the Palace is the **Round Pond** **16** , a 7-acre (2.8ha) ornamental lake created in 1730 by George II, popular with model yacht enthusiasts (and waterfowl!).

The Orangery

Walk 1

Just past the Palace is **The Orangery** 17 , once the setting for Queen Anne's sophisticated court entertainment, with its soaring ceilings and classical 18th-century architecture; today, it's a restaurant, and a spectacular setting for breakfast, lunch or afternoon tea. A little further on, in the northwest corner of the gardens, is the **Diana, Princess of Wales Memorial Playground** 18 , opened in 2000. Nearby you find the **Elfin Oak** 19 (1930) – a much-loved sculpture made from the hollow trunk of an oak tree, carved with fairies, elves and animals – and Time Flies, a clock tower and drinking fountain.

Food & Drink

⑤ **Serpentine Bar & Kitchen:** This iconic café/ restaurant serves delicious seasonal English classics (8am-6/7pm, £-££).

⑧ **Lido Bar & Café:** Enjoy a cuppa or a glass of wine overlooking the Serpentine (8am-8pm, £).

⑰ **Orangery Restaurant:** From Shetland salmon to Cornish yogurt, thoroughly British fare served up in Queen Anne's magnificent greenhouse (10am-6pm, £-££).

㉗ **Magazine Restaurant:** The stunning restaurant in the Serpentine Sackler Gallery is the perfect setting in which to enjoy contemporary European cuisine (9am-6pm. closed Mon, £-££).

Physical Energy

Retrace your steps back past the clock tower and take the first path on the left, passing the Round Pond on your right, heading for the centre of the gardens and the impressive **Physical Energy Statue** 20 by George Frederic Watts, OM RA (1817-1904). The large bronze sculpture depicts a naked man, astride a horse, shielding his eyes from the sun and is based on an equestrian monument Watts made in 1870 of Hugh Lupus, an ancestor of the Duke of Westminster. Take the second of the two paths leading left from the statue and at the next junction, a short way ahead, turn sharp right towards the Long Water. This quiet and secluded part of the gardens has some particularly attractive trees, some of them intriguingly gnarled and mangled by time, wind and lightning strikes.

The path continues to the left with the **Long Water** ㉑, the northern 'tail' of the Serpentine, on your right. Look out for the famous bronze **statue of Peter Pan** ㉒ (see box) on the left overlooking the lake – playing his pipe, surrounded by fairies and woodland creatures – in a part of the gardens that's rich in birdlife, including ducks and herons.

Just ahead, opposite the Italian Gardens, is the much loved **Two Bears Fountain** ㉓, featuring a statue of two bears embracing. It was installed in 1939 to mark 80 years of the Metropolitan Drinking Fountain and Cattle Trough Association, which promoted temperance, i.e. abstinence from alcohol, as well as providing water for animals.

The splendid **Italian Gardens** ㉔ at the top of the Long Water is an ornamental water garden – created in 1860 to a design by James Pennethorne at the instigation of Prince Albert – an enchanting over-the-top confection of fountains, urns and classical sculptures carved in Carrara marble. There's also an Italian summerhouse and Queen

Peter Pan Statue

Erected in 1912, the statue by Sir George Frampton was commissioned and paid for by J.M. Barrie, creator of Peter Pan (the 'boy who wouldn't grow up'). Barrie chose the location himself, claiming it's the spot where Peter landed in *Peter Pan in Kensington Gardens*. Today, it's one of London's most popular statues, beloved by generations of children.

Anne's Alcove, designed by Sir Christopher Wren in 1705. Look out for Albert and Victoria's initials carved on the wall of the pump house, which contained the steam engine that powered the fountains. Follow the path around the eastern side of the Long Water, where there's a large bronze **statue of Jenner** ㉕; Dr Edward Jenner (1749-1823) was the pioneer of the smallpox vaccine and is often called 'the father of immunology'. The statue, by W. Calder Marshall, was originally erected in Trafalgar Square in 1858, before being moved here in 1862.

Follow the path south along the Long Water in an area called Buckhill, passing the Buckhill Shelter on the Peacock Walk, until you come to the **Henry Moore Arch** ㉖ sited alongside the lake. This 20ft (6m) travertine marble sculpture (weighing 37 tons) was donated by Moore in 1980, and perfectly frames a view of Kensington Palace. Just past the

Italian Gardens

The first-ever Victoria Cross investiture took place in Hyde Park on 26th June 1857, when 62 heroes of the Crimean War were decorated by Queen Victoria in the presence of Prince Albert and other members of the royal family.

Serpentine Sackler Gallery

statue you reach the Magazine Gate, Serpentine Bridge and the **Serpentine Sackler Gallery** ㉗, a sister gallery of the Serpentine Gallery you visited earlier. Designed by the late Zaha Hadid (1950-2016), the striking gallery is housed in a former 1805 gunpowder store and opened in 2013. The Sackler presents world-renowned exhibitions of art, architecture and design throughout the year (entrance is free and there's also a fine restaurant). Nearby is the Allotment, where visitors can garner useful tips about growing fruit and vegetables.

Take the main path behind the Gallery and follow the Policeman's Path, with the Central Royal Parks Nursery on your left, to the **Old Police House** ㉘. Built in 1900 as the headquarters of the Royal Parks police force, it's now part of a group of buildings that include the Ranger's Lodge & Cottage, Serpentine Lodge and the Royal Parks HQ & Information Centre (020-7298 2100). At the crossroads continue straight ahead to the **Reformers' Tree** ㉙, a circular black and white mosaic (2000) that marks the spot where the original Reformers' Tree stood. This noble oak was the focus of protests in 1866 by the Reform League, campaigning for all adult men to be given the right to vote.

From the mosaic take the diagonal path northeast towards **Marble Arch** ㉚, a white Carrara marble monument designed by John Nash, which stands on a traffic island just outside the park at the junction of Oxford Street and Park Lane, almost directly opposite **Speakers' Corner** ㉛ (see box). Completed in 1833, the arch stood in front of Buckingham Palace until 1851, when it was moved here. In front of the Arch is a changing display of statues,

Still Water

Speakers' Corner

although it's the permanent location for **Still Water 32**, a giant bronze horse's head (33ft/10m, weighing 6 tons) by Nic Fiddian-Green, installed in 2009. As you stand here, take a moment to reflect on the 50,000 people who lost their lives near this spot, for this was the site of the infamous Tyburn Gallows, and a place of execution from 1196 to 1783. To the north of the park (at 8 Hyde Park Place), the Tyburn Convent is dedicated to the memory of martyrs executed here (and elsewhere) for their Catholic faith.

Continue south along the Broad Walk, which runs parallel to Park Lane, and just outside the park (on the central reservation, opposite Upper Brook Street) – a short distance past the kiosk – is one of London's most poignant memorials. The **Animals in War Memorial 33** by David Backhouse is a tribute to the millions of animals that served, suffered and died alongside the British, Commonwealth and Allied forces in the wars and conflicts of the 20th century. It features two heavily-laden mules trudging towards an opening between two swelling Portland stone screens,

beyond which lies a grass mound with a cavorting horse and a dog. Park Lane has been a sought-after and upmarket address since the 1820s and remains one of London's most fashionable streets. However, in the 20th century many of the great houses that once lined the road were demolished and it's now mainly home to offices and hotels, including the Dorchester and Hilton.

Joy of Life Fountain

Some 400m further on you come to the **Joy of Life Fountain** , also known as the Four Winds Fountain, by T. B. Huxley-Jones. Unveiled in 1963, it was donated by the Constance Fund – an organisation founded by the painter and art patron Sigismund Christian Hubert Goetze (1866-1939) and named after his wife Constance – which encouraged art sculptures in London parks. The fountain features two bronze figures holding hands seeming to dance above the water, while four children emerge from the pool. Around 60,000 daffodil bulbs are planted near the fountain, creating a spectacular display in early spring. Continue south along the Broad Walk for around 300m and you pass the **7th July Memorial** 35, a short distance to the left off the main path. The memorial honours the victims of the London Bombings on 7th July 2005 – each

Pet Cemetery 38

In the garden of Victoria Gate Lodge, just off Bayswater Road (near Lancaster Gate tube station), is one of Hyde Park's curiosities: a pint-sized cemetery full of miniature headstones. It's the last resting place of over 300 much-loved pets – mainly dogs – buried between 1881 and 1903. The first dog interred, a Maltese called Cherry, belonged to friends of the gatekeeper, Mr Winbridge. The epitaphs are heartfelt, even if some names are strange: 'residents' include Fattie, Tally-Ho and Pomme de Terre! Sadly, the cemetery can only be viewed through the railings or by appointment. Today, it serves as a touching reminder of the special relationship that exists between animals and humans.

of the 52 stainless steel pillars represents one of those killed in the atrocity.

As you return to your starting point at Hyde Park Corner, on your left is the imposing bronze **Statue of Achilles** 36, standing 18ft (5.5m) tall and made from cannons captured during the Duke of Wellington's campaigns in France. The Greek hero of the Trojan War carries a sword and shield with his armour beside him, although his head is said to be modelled on the Duke of Wellington. Sculpted by Richard Westmacott, it was unveiled in 1822 and was the first statue

Achilles

installed in Hyde Park. It was also London's first public naked statue and caused considerable controversy, a fig leaf being added later to cover Achilles' appendage (it isn't recorded whether this, too, was modelled on the Duke's).

To the right of the statue is the magnificent **Queen Elizabeth Gate** 37, unveiled in 1993 to commemorate the 90th birthday of Queen Elizabeth the Queen Mother (it's also known as the Queen Mother's Gate). The gate railings and lamps are by Giuseppe Lund and made of forged stainless steel and bronze, while the central screen is by David Wynne.

Queen Elizabeth Gate

As you exit the gates and head back to the tube station at one of London's busiest junctions, it's difficult to imagine how it appeared many centuries ago, when Kensington and Knightsbridge were just small villages and a tollgate on this spot marked the western entrance to London.

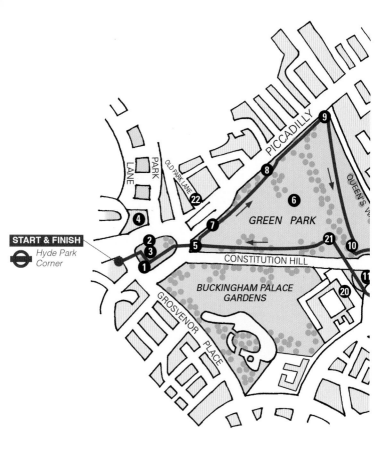

1 Wellington Arch

2 Statue of Wellington

3 Military Memorials

4 Apsley House

5 Memorial Gates

6 Green Park

7 RAF Bomber Command Memorial

8 Devonshire Gates

9 Constance Fund Fountain

10 Canada Gate

11 Queen Victoria Memorial

12 St James's Park

13 Blue Bridge

14 Swire Fountain

15 Duck Island

16 St James's Café

17 Guards Memorial

18 Tiffany Fountain

● Places of Interest ● Food & Drink

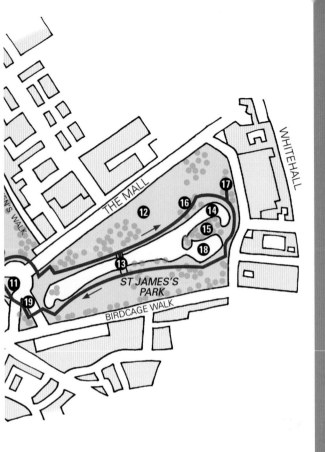

Green Park & St James's Park

WALK 2

ℹ

Distance: 3mi (4.8km)

Terrain: easy

Duration: 1½ hours

Open: Green Park (unrestricted), St James's Park (5am to midnight)

Start & End: Hyde Park Corner tube

Postcode: SW1X 7LY

This walk takes in the two smallest London royal parks, although they are only small in comparison with the vastness of the city's other royal parks, and what they lack in size they more than make up for in beauty, particularly St James's Park.

Green Park – its name reflects its verdant grass and mature trees (mostly limes and plane trees, but also some black poplar trees) – is the smallest of London's royal parks (47 acres/19ha). Some people find it rather austere – it's now devoid of buildings, but it once contained lodges, a library, an ice house and two vast 'temples' (the Temples of Peace and Concord) – but it's a peaceful refuge and particularly popular for sunbathing and picnics. Henry VIII enclosed the park in the 16th century and it was a famous duelling spot until 1667, when Charles II purchased an extra 40 acres and it became known as upper St James's Park (it was officially renamed Green Park in 1746). The park was opened to the public in 1826.

Slightly larger than Green Park at 57 acres (23ha), St James's Park is London's oldest royal park. It's named after St James the Less, one of the 12 Apostles, to whom the first building on the site – St James's Hospital for female lepers – was dedicated; it was rebuilt in 1531-36 as St James's Palace and remains a royal residence to this day. The park was originally a marshy field by the hospital where the lepers fed their pigs, but Henry VIII had it drained to use as a nursery for his deer. James I kept a menagerie in the park, including camels, crocodiles and elephants, as well as an aviary of exotic birds on what is now Birdcage Walk.

The park's centrepiece is a tranquil lake with small islands at either end, surrounded by lawns and ancient trees, plus the requisite bandstand and deckchairs. It's the only large London park that isn't enclosed by railings and is considered by many to be the most beautiful of the Royal Parks due to its views, waterfowl and flower displays.

Start Walking...

Leaving Hyde Park Corner tube station, it's worth investigating the area around Hyde Park Corner before entering Green Park. Cross the road to the large island in the middle of this busy traffic intersection, which contains a number of interesting monuments. The largest and most imposing are the **Wellington Arch** ❶ (see box) and, in front of it, the **Statue of Wellington** ❷. The bronze statue, set on a polished granite plinth, is by Sir Joseph Edgar Boehm (1888). It depicts the Iron Duke in uniform on his favourite horse, Copenhagen, while at each corner are bronze figures of soldiers from various regiments.

The island also contains a number of other fine **Memorials** ❸: the Royal Artillery Memorial,

---

Wellington Arch

Designed by Decimus Burton, the Arch was built in 1826-30 to commemorate Wellington's victory over Napoleon at the Battle of Waterloo. It was originally crowned with a massive statue of the Duke that stood 28ft (8.5m) high and weighed 40 tons, but this attracted ridicule as its vast size made the Arch look like a footstool! The controversial statue was removed to Aldershot after the Duke's death and replaced in 1912 by a large bronze quadriga (a chariot drawn by four horses) – Europe's largest bronze sculpture – depicting the angel of peace descending on the chariot of war. In contrast to its flamboyant decoration, the Arch itself is surprisingly plain, as much of the intended exterior decoration was omitted in order to save money after George IV overspent on the refurbishment of Buckingham Palace. The Arch is now owned by English Heritage and has exhibits detailing its history (see www.english-heritage. org.uk/visit/places/wellington-arch for information) and visitors can climb to the top where there are terraces on both sides affording panoramic views over London. Creative floodlighting makes the Arch an impressive sight at night.

---

the Machine Gun Corps Memorial, the Australian War Memorial and the New Zealand War Memorial, commemorating soldiers who fell in the two World Wars. The imposing Royal Artillery Memorial (to the right of the Arch) by Charles Jagger and Lionel Pearson features a giant sculpture of a howitzer upon a large plinth surrounded by four bronze figures of artillery men, in stark contrast to the Machine Gun Corps Memorial – opposite Wellington Arch – which features a 9ft (2.7m) bronze statue of a naked David by Francis

Wellington Arch

Apsley House

Also known as Number 1 London, Apsley House was the first house visitors saw when passing through the tollgate at Knightsbridge. It was originally built for Lord Apsley by Robert Adam in 1771-8 and was acquired in 1817 by the Duke of Wellington, who faced the red brick walls with Bath stone. Grade I listed and run by English Heritage, it's now a museum and art gallery (Wed-Sun, 11am-5pm, weekends only in summer), although the current Duke still uses part of the building as his London residence. The interior has changed little since the Iron Duke's time and is a dazzling example of the Regency style. There's also a fine art collection, including works by Bruegel the Elder, Goya, Landseer, Murillo, Rubens, Van Dyck and Velázquez. For information see www.english-heritage.org.uk/visit/places/apsley-house.

RAF Bomber Command Memorial

From the traffic island, cross the road at the lights opposite Constitution Hill and ahead of you are the pillars of the **Memorial Gates ❺** by Liam O'Connor. Unveiled in 2002, they're inscribed: 'In memory of the five million volunteers from the Indian sub-continent, Africa and the Caribbean who fought with Britain in the two world wars'. Here you turn left and enter **Green Park ❻**, walking towards Piccadilly; after 100m or so you come to the magnificent **RAF Bomber Command Memorial ❼**, London's newest – and long overdue – war memorial. It was only unveiled in 2012 and marks the sacrifice of 55,573 aircrew, from Britain, Czechoslovakia, Poland, Canada and other Commonwealth countries, who were killed during air-raids in World War Two. The monument

Derwent Wood, with one hand on his hip and the other resting on Goliath's oversized sword. On the other side of Piccadilly is attractive, honey-coloured **Apsley House ❹**, the former home of the Duke of Wellington (see box).

Apsley House

There are no formal flowerbeds in Green Park. This is reputedly due to instructions from Catherine of Braganza, wife of Charles II, who on discovering that the king had picked flowers in the park and given them to another woman, ordered that every single flower be uprooted and no more planted. However, nowadays it has thousands of daffodils in spring.

Queen Victoria Memorial

Sculpted by Sir Thomas Brock and unveiled by King George V in 1911, this imposing imperial memorial commemorates Queen Victoria (1819-1901) and the glory days of the British Empire. The statue of the Queen is over 18ft (5.5m) high and cut from a single block of white Carrara marble, while the whole monument stands at 82ft (25m) and comprises 2,300 tons of marble. Many allegorical figures accompany Victoria, representing courage, constancy, victory, charity, truth and motherhood. The empire's three most important dominions – Canada, Australia and South and West Africa – are celebrated in ornamental gates on the roads encircling the monument, which are adorned with cherubs bearing appropriate symbols including a Merino sheep for Australia, a net full of fish for Canada and an ostrich for Africa. The overall design of the monument was conceived by Sir Aston Webb and includes the Memorial Gardens, a broad semi-circular sweep of flowerbeds enclosed by a low stone balustrade.

your left, which were installed here in 1921. The fine early 18th-century wrought iron ornamental gates and Palladian gate piers of Portland stone originate from Lord Heathfield's house in Turnham Green, west London. At the end of the path you reach the northeast corner (the Green Park tube station entrance) of the park and the **Constance Fund Fountain** ❾ by Jim Clack – also known as the Diana Fountain as it depicts the goddess Diana – unveiled in 2011.

Canada Gate

From the fountain take the well-worn diagonal path leading south to Buckingham Palace. After around 5 minutes, at the end of the path, is the striking golden **Canada Gate** ❿, which forms a grand entrance to the park and the tree-lined Broad Walk. The gates were a gift from Canada to celebrate its contribution to the British Empire and were installed in 1911 as part of the memorial to Queen Victoria. Designed by Sir Aston Webb, they are in the same style as those of Buckingham Palace and bear the emblems of the seven Canadian provinces of

features a striking 9ft (2.7m) bronze sculpture by Philip Jackson depicting aircrew returning from a bombing mission.

Continue along the path which runs parallel to Piccadilly in the direction of the Broad Walk along a lovely avenue of oak trees. After a few hundred metres you pass the **Devonshire Gates** ❽ on

Food & Drink

- **Kiosks:** These can be found at Marlborough Gate, Horse Shoe Bend, Artillery Memorial, and the playground – serving sandwiches, snacks, ice cream, coffee and cold drinks (9am-4/8pm, £).

16 St James's Café: Overlooking Duck Island, this café/restaurant serves a wide-ranging British menu. It also offers a 'grab and go' menu, so you can take away treats for a picnic (8am-4/10pm, 9am-4/10pm Sun, £).

22 The Rose & Crown: Dating back over 400 years, this traditional pub at 2 Old Park Lane is a good choice for a drink or lunch before or after your walk (11am or noon-11pm, £).

the time. Opposite Canada Gate on the roundabout and directly in front of Buckingham Palace is the magnificent **Queen Victoria Memorial** 11 (see box).

From Canada Gate turn left, skirting the Memorial Gardens, and cross over The Mall and enter **St James's Park** 12 via the entrance a few metres up on the right. The park is long and narrow with a lake

running down the middle. Plantings include the Nash shrubberies and the 'tropical' border, both on the north side of the lake. The majority of trees in the park are plane trees, which are known for their flaking bark and resistance to pollution. Other species include the black mulberry, which was associated with James I's failed attempt to create a British silk industry, and fig trees which border the lake.

From the entrance, continue straight ahead (past a kiosk on your right) to the lake. West Island – one of two small islands on the lake – is directly in front of you. The lake is home to a wealth of waterfowl, including the famous pelicans, mallards, tufted duck, shelduck, wigeon, gadwall, teal, pintail, shoveler, common pochard, red-crested pochard, goldeneye, coot, moorhen, little grebe, great crested grebe, Canada geese, greylag geese, mute and black swans, and grey herons.

Bear left following the path along the edge of the lake to the **Blue Bridge** 13; the original elegant suspension bridge was built across the lake in 1857, but was replaced a century later by a concrete crossing. From here you can enjoy some of London's best views: west for Buckingham Palace and the Victoria Memorial framed by trees, east for Horse Guards Parade and the towers, turrets, spires and domes of Whitehall.

Continue along the path, passing the bandstand on the left (there are deckchairs for hire and free concerts on summer evenings), until you reach the **Swire Fountain** 14 in the lake; installed in 2007, its jets reach over 15ft (4.5m) high. Behind the fountain, in the middle of the lake, is **Duck Island** 15. It's attached to the park by an isthmus (so not really an island) and is a sanctuary for birdlife, including St James's famous colony of pelicans – the original birds were a gift from Russia in the 17th century – if you arrive between 2.30 and 3.30pm you may see them being fed. A few steps to the left is **St James's Café** 16, a peaceful setting in which to enjoy breakfast or lunch. Surrounded by an abundance of flora and fauna, it offers fine views of the lake and fountain from the contemporary roof terrace, external seating areas and the panoramic floor-to-ceiling windows.

> The Mall, and nearby Pall Mall, get their name from a game which Charles II introduced from France, which was played on courts in St James's Park. Pele Mele, a forerunner of croquet, was played on a long fenced court, using a mallet to hit a ball through a hoop.

The path leads around the top of the eastern edge of the lake, but it's worth making a short detour to see the **Guards Memorial** 17 off to the left. Facing Horse Guards Parade, the memorial by Gilbert Ledward was unveiled in 1926 and commemorates the guardsmen who died in World War One. In the form of a cenotaph, it features five life-size bronze figures each representing one of the five Foot Guards' Regiments (Grenadiers, Coldstream, Scots, Welsh and Irish).

Green Park

Buckingham Palace

As you continue around the end of the lake, past Duck Island Cottage and garden – built for the park's bird keeper in 1841 in the design of a Swiss chalet – the **Tiffany Fountain** 18 comes into view. At the centre of the lake in front of Duck Island, the fountain sends a 20ft (6m) plume of water into the air, enhancing the spectacular views. On special occasions the jet is illuminated at night in any one of a rainbow spectrum of colours. Walk along the southern edge of the lake – which runs parallel to Birdcage Walk – and you soon find yourself back at the Blue Bridge. Continue past the bridge until you reach the western end of the lake opposite Buckingham Palace. There's a kiosk here where you can get a drink or snack.

Exit St James's Park onto Birdcage Walk and cross the road, passing **Australia Gate** 19 on your right, which is opposite Canada Gate that you saw earlier. The route takes you in front of

Buckingham Palace 20, the London residence of HM Queen Elizabeth II, where if you're lucky and time it right (around 11am most days), you can see the Changing of the Guard (see http://changing-guard.com for the schedule).

Cross over Constitution Hill (see box) and follow the path directly ahead into Green Park (passing a kiosk on the right just past the Canada Gate) and take the second path on the left, which leads to the **Canada Memorial** 21 on your right, which commemorates the 113,663 Canadians who died in the two world wars. Designed by Canadian Pierre Granche, it's made from red granite and is divided by a walkway into two distinct halves, representing participation in World Wars One and Two. The inclined sculpture is inset with bronze maple leaves (the Canadian emblem) and the country's coat of arms; water flows across the sloping surface and creates an illusion of floating leaves.

Return to the main path and take the diagonal path off to the left, which takes you back to your starting point at Hyde Park Corner. If you feel like some liquid refreshment after your walk, try the historic **Rose & Crown** 22 pub – once the living quarters for Oliver Cromwell's bodyguards – at 2 Old Park Lane (off the north side of Piccadilly just past the Hard Rock Café). A bit further along Piccadilly, at the corner of Down Street, is the spectacular Athenaeum Hotel vertical garden.

Constitution Hill

Constitution Hill – which isn't a hill at all – dates from the 17th century and the reign of King Charles II, who was said to take his 'daily constitutional' walks along the route with his favourite spaniels. Other monarchs found it a dangerous place: three attempts were made on Queen Victoria's life while travelling along Constitution Hill, in 1840, 1842 and 1849. It now divides Green Park from Buckingham Palace's walled gardens and is lined with splendid plane trees.

St James's Park

1 Regent's Park

2 Clarence Gate & Bridge

3 Bandstand

4 Inner Circle

5 Regent's Bar & Kitchen

6 Jubilee Gates

7 Japanese Garden Island

8 Queen Mary's Rose Gardens

9 Triton Fountain

10 The Boy and Frog Statue

11 Open Air Theatre

12 St John's Lodge Garden

13 Awakening Statue

14 Boating Lake

15 Wildlife & Waterfowl Centre

16 Hanover Bridges & Hanover Island

17 Boathouse Café

18 Hub Sports Centre

19 London Zoo

20 The Broad Walk

21 Ready Money Drinking Fountain

22 The Smokehouse

23 The Espresso Bar

24 Avenue Gardens

25 Griffin Tazza

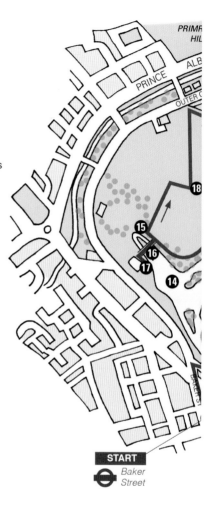

START

Baker Street

Places of Interest   Food & Drink

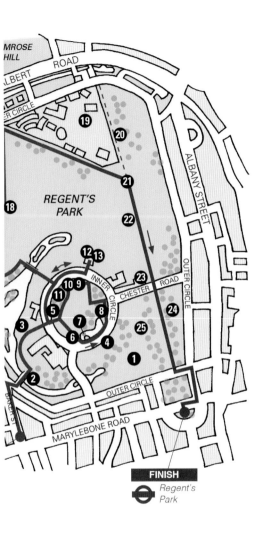

Regent's Park

Distance: 4mi (6.4km)
Terrain: easy, mostly flat
Duration: 2 hours
Open: 5am to dusk
Start: Baker Street tube
End: Regent's Park tube
Postcode: NW1 5LA

REGENT'S PARK

A vast swathe of parkland bounded by some of the UK's most exquisite Georgian terraces, Regent's Park is the largest of central London's five royal parks at 410 acres (166ha). It's also home to the internationally renowned London Zoo. A masterpiece of landscape design and town planning, it was created in the early 19th century for the Prince Regent – later George IV – and is officially titled *The* Regent's Park. Nowadays it's perhaps best known for its sporting and entertainment facilities, although it's also a good place to appreciate nature in the capital, particularly its wealth of birdlife, with a diverse range of environments including woodland (majestic trees!) and wetland, open meadows and exquisite formal gardens.

Regent's Park has an unusual layout consisting of two ring roads: the Outer and Inner Circles. The Inner Circle encloses formal gardens and an open-air theatre, while the Outer Circle borders the outer reaches of the park and its many amenities, which include gardens, a lake, sports pitches, playgrounds and a zoo. To the north, the park's perimeter is delimited by Regent's Canal (Walk 7), built to link the Grand Union Canal to the London Docks; the canal divides the main park from Primrose Hill, officially part of Regent's Park but which most Londoners consider to be a separate park.

Like many of London's royal parks, the land which now forms Regent's Park was appropriated from its ecclesiastical owners – in this case the nuns of Barking Abbey – by Henry VIII, who used it for hunting deer. When hunting fell out of fashion in the mid-17th century it was leased as farmland. It wasn't until 1811 that the architect John Nash (1752-1835) was commissioned by the Prince Regent to transform the area into a fashionable suburb around the park.

Plant lovers should note that Regent's Park has some glorious formal gardens, including Queen Mary's Rose Gardens within the Inner Circle, the Avenue Gardens in the south-eastern corner and the 'secret' Garden of St John's Lodge, all of which feature in this walk.

Start Walking…

Leaving Baker Street tube, take the exit for Baker Street (not Marylebone Road), turn right and cross over the Outer Circle to enter **Regent's Park ❶** via **Clarence Gate & Bridge ❷**. Turn left across the bridge and continue straight ahead with the Boating Lake on your left. After a few minutes you'll pass the **Bandstand ❸** on Holme Green, where visitors can enjoy a variety of lunchtime and evening concerts. In 1982, the band of the Royal Green Jackets was the target of an IRA terrorist bomb, which left seven soldiers dead and 24 injured. A small plaque on the bandstand commemorates the victims of the attack. Just ahead is the entrance to the **Inner Circle ❹**. On your left just after you enter the Circle is the **Regent's Bar & Kitchen** 5 (formerly called the Garden Café), which is the perfect place for morning coffee or a spot of lunch.

> ### Queen Mary's Rose Gardens
>
> Named after the wife of George V, the gardens were laid out in 1932 and contain London's largest and best formal rose garden. They're a honeypot for garden lovers (and bees) in spring and summer, when thousands of plants are in bloom. As well as the glorious roses, these delightful gardens feature the national collection of delphiniums and some 9,000 begonias, laid out in landscaped beds surrounded by a ring of pillars covered in climbers and ramblers. **No dogs are permitted in the gardens.**

After passing the Regent's Bar continue ahead to the right and follow the path round past the main entrance with its **Jubilee Gates ❻**. The grand iron and gilded semi-circular gates were installed to mark the Silver Jubilee

Queen Mary's Rose Gardens

of King George V and the official opening of the gardens in 1935. Follow the path along the edge of the lake, with its ornamental ducks and carp, until you come to the **Japanese Garden Island ❼**. Cross to the island over the wooden bow bridge (covered in

35

Walk 3

wisteria in spring) and follow the path round to the right, passing a large eagle sculpture, to the other side, where there's a stunning tumbling waterfall opposite the island.

Return to the path via the bridge and a short way past the lake are the magnificent **Queen Mary's Rose Gardens** ❽ (see box). In summer, rose lovers will be in raptures, enveloped by the intoxicating sight and scent of thousands of blooms (the best time to visit is the first two weeks of June). There are around 12,000 roses planted in the gardens, including 85 single variety beds. The garden artfully combines the formal, academic planting of single variety beds with the charm of climbing and rambling roses around the circular borders, with gorgeous vistas of green lawns and the tranquil lake beyond. Benches are strategically placed among the roses for quiet enjoyment of the views and fragrance.

Triton Fountain

St John's Lodge Garden

An exquisite quintessential English garden, that's secreted down a pergola-draped path, completely separate from the lodge. Open to the public since 1928, the garden is managed and maintained by the Royal Parks. It was designed by Robert Weir Schultz in 1892 for the 3rd Marquess of Bute, and includes formal areas, a fountain pond, statues, a Doric temple, stone portico and partly sunken chapel, reflecting the Arts and Crafts ideas popular at the time, as well as the revival of interest in classical themes. New planting in the '90s further enhanced the garden, which is an unexpected treat. A popular bronze, **Awakening** ⓭ by Wuts Safardier, dedicated to Anne Lydia Evans, is located at the front right section of the garden.

After you've had your fill of roses, follow the path ahead and turn left at the end (the eastern entrance to the Inner Circle is on the right) and then right towards the top of the gardens and the beautiful **Triton Fountain** ❾. It has pride of place at the top of the wide path which runs from the main gates. Designed by William McMillan RA (1887-1977), the fountain was donated in 1950 in memory of the artist Sigismund Goetze (1866-1939) by his wife Constance. In a nearby pond is the **Boy and Frog Statue** ❿ by Sir William Reid Dick (1936), a bronze figure of a boy and a frog on a pedestal of Finnish granite, donated by Sigismund Goetze himself (a patron of the park).

Continue round the Inner Circle in an anti-clockwise direction and you come to the **Open Air Theatre** ⓫, a permanent venue founded in 1932 with a three- to four-month summer season (http://openairtheatre.com). The steep auditorium seats 1,240 and boasts one of the longest 'bars' in any theatre in London, stretching the entire length of the seating (meals are served from 90 minutes before performances and during the interval). A grill is also provided (you can save by pre-purchasing a voucher) plus pre-ordered picnics and hampers.

A disaster overtook skaters on the lake in Regent's Park on 15th January 1867, when the ice gave way plunging hundreds of people into 12ft (3.7m) of icy water. Bystanders tore branches off trees and launched boats in a desperate rescue attempt, but despite their efforts 40 people lost their lives. To prevent a similar catastrophe happening again, the water was drained and the lake bed raised with soil and concrete, and it's now just 4ft (1.2m) deep.

St John's Lodge Garden

Carry on south along the path and leave the Inner Circle where you entered, just past the café, and turn right to head north with the Holme mansion – designed by Decimus Burton in 1818 – on your left. A little further on you pass a path to the left leading to the Long Bridge and the Boating Lake, which we'll return to later, but for now go straight ahead around the Circle. Just past the top of the Inner Circle take the 'hidden' paved arbour path on the left (it's easy to miss it!) leading to the enchanting **St John's Lodge Garden** ⑫ (see box).

The imposing Lodge of 1817-19 was the first house to be built in Regent's Park. Designed by John Raffield for Charles Augustus Tulk MP, it was one of over 50 great villas envisaged by John Nash in a plan to transform the park and surrounding area in the 1800s. Sadly, only eight villas were built.

Retrace your steps round the Inner Circle and take the path on the right leading to the **Boating Lake** ⑭ and the Long Bridge. The lake is a tricorn shape with bridges at each 'corner'. You can hire a boat or pedalo from the Boathouse (April to October) or do a spot of bird watching; just north of the Long Bridge is a wetland area, goose grazing pen and waterfowl collection. After crossing the bridge turn left and follow the

One of the Hanover Bridges

Food & Drink

5 **Regent's Bar & Kitchen:**
The original '60s park
café has been refurbished
and offers drinks, lunches
and suppers in the lush
surroundings of Queen
Mary's Rose Gardens in
the Inner Circle (8am to
9pm, 6pm in winter, £).

17 **Boathouse Café**: With a
large terrace overlooking
the Boating Lake – from
where you can watch the
antics of the waterfowl
– the Boathouse serves
pizza, pasta and other
family favourites (from
9am, closing time varies,
£).

22 **Smokehouse**: Hot food,
summer salads, ice cream
and more. Located north
of the Espresso Bar on the
Broad Walk on the eastern
side of the park (8am to
4pm, £).

23 **Espresso Bar**: Located
on the Broad Walk
at Chester Road, the
Espresso offers farm-
made dairy ice cream,
real milk shakes, cream
scones, sandwiches and
treats (8am to 4pm, £).

north shore of the lake until you
reach the **Wildlife & Waterfowl
Centre** **15** on your right (no public
access) and **Hanover Bridges &
Hanover Island** **16** on the left.
Cross the bridges (there are a
pair) to the **Boathouse Café** **17** ,
a family restaurant with a large
terrace seating area overlooking
the lake.

London Zoo

From the Boathouse, cross
back over the Hanover Bridges
and take the path north towards
London Zoo, passing **The Hub
Sports Centre** **18** on your
right in the centre of the park.
It's the largest outdoor sports
facility in London, complete with
underground changing rooms
and a café. As well as outdoor
exercise classes and children's
activities, it maintains pitches for
soccer, rugby, lacrosse, softball
and cricket. A few hundred metres
north of The Hub is **London
Zoo** **19** , the world's oldest
scientific zoo housing one of the
largest collections of animals in
the world (around 700 species).
Favourite residents include
penguins, gorillas and a family of
meerkats, and the zoo features
iconic architecture such as the

Mappin Terraces (1913) and Lord Snowdon's Aviary (1962). For more information and ticket prices, see www.zsl.org/zsl-london-zoo.

From the Zoo head towards the **Broad Walk** 20 on the eastern side of the park – lined with chestnuts and maples – where you find the **Ready Money Drinking Fountain** 21 , a four-sided granite and marble gothic drinking fountain. It gets its unusual name from Sir Cowasjee Jehangir, a Parsee industrialist whose nickname was Ready Money and who donated it to the park in 1869. Continue south on the Broad Walk, passing the **Smokehouse** 22 to your right and **The Espresso Bar** 23 at the end, both good places to refuel.

Just south of the Broad Walk in the south-eastern corner of the park are the sumptuous **Avenue Gardens** 24 , a treasure trove of elegant displays of spring bulbs and summer bedding, with tiered fountains, evergreen hedges and vast ornamental bowls overflowing with flowers. In the centre stands a large circular stone bowl supported by four winged stone lions, known as the **Griffin Tazza** 25 – also called the Lion Vase – installed by landscape architect William Andrews Nesfield in 1863. The gardens are the venue for some excellent sculpture exhibitions, including the annual Frieze Sculpture (July to October).

Avenue Gardens

Leaving the park, head south and follow Park Square West – sadly, the central gardens are only accessible to key holders – and cross Marylebone Road to Regent's Park tube station, and the end of the walk.

1 Design Museum
2 Wrought Iron Gates
3 Youth Hostel
4 Holland House
5 Gate Piers
6 Café
7 The Maid Statue
8 Sun God Statue
9 Ice House
10 Sibirica Fountain
11 Belvedere Restaurant
12 Orangery
13 Wrestlers of Herculaneum
14 Boy with Bear Cubs Statue
15 Dutch Garden
16 Wall Trough
17 Ancient Melancholy Man Statue
18 Milo of Croton Statue
19 Armillary Sphere
20 Napoleon Garden

● Places of Interest ● Food & Drink

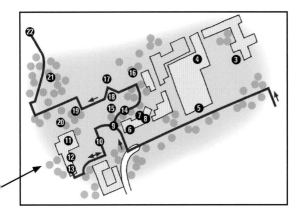

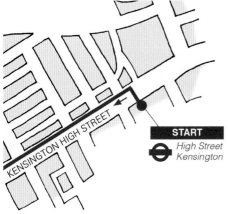

START
High Street
Kensington

WALK 4

21 Walking Man Sculpture

22 Kyoto Garden

23 Ecology Centre

24 Adventure Playground

25 Tortoises with Triangle & Time Sculpture

26 Wildlife Enclosures

27 Henry Richard Vassal Fox, 3rd Baron Holland Memorial

28 Sun Trap Entrance

29 Mitre Pub

Holland Park & Kyoto Garden

Distance: 2mi (3.2km)

Terrain: easy

Duration: 1hr

Open: 7.30am to dusk

Start: High Street Kensington tube

End: Holland Park tube

Postcode: W8 5SA

Holland Park – managed by the Royal Borough of Kensington and Chelsea – is considered by many to be London's most romantic park. At 54 acres (22ha) it's the borough's largest park and has plenty to offer: beautiful views, glorious gardens, a wealth of statuary, galleries, sports facilities, an ecology centre, some of London's best children's play facilities, a restaurant and café, large areas of woodland, a pride of peacocks and a stunning Japanese garden. The park is also a favourite picnic spot, with plenty of secluded hideaways in a variety of environments.

Holland Park was previously the grounds of Cope Castle, later renamed Holland House, a large early 17th-century Jacobean mansion. It was one of the area's first great houses with an estate of some 500 acres (202ha) stretching from Holland Park Avenue to today's Earl's Court tube station. The area remained a rural backwater until the 19th century, when the owners began to sell off parts of the estate for residential development, and the district that evolved took its name from the house.

Holland House was almost totally destroyed during the Blitz; the ruins and grounds were purchased in 1952 from the 6th Earl of Ilchester by London County Council to create a public park. Today, the park comprises three distinct areas: the northern half is semi-wild woodland (including a wildlife or 'nature' reserve with limited public access) where the sounds of the city all but disappear; the central part – around the remains of Holland House – is more formal, with a number of gardens; and the southern section is used mainly for sport (facilities include tennis courts, soccer pitches, golf and cricket practice nets, and a netball court). Holland Park is also home to an arts venue with two gallery spaces (the Orangery and Ice House), an open-air theatre and contemporary sculpture exhibitions in the Napoleon Garden.

Start Walking…

From Kensington High Street tube station, turn left up Kensington High Street and cross over the road. The entrance to Holland Park is around 500m up on your right. But first, you may wish to drop into the **Design Museum** ❶ (see box), adjacent to the park.

Design Museum

London's principal design museum covers product, industrial, graphic, fashion and architectural design; it relocated here (to the former Commonwealth Institute building) in 2016 from Shad Thames in southeast London. The dramatic £83 million development – with its distinctive copper-covered roof – was designed by John Pawson. Entrance to the museum's permanent collection display 'Designer Maker User' is free, although there's a fee to see temporary exhibitions. There's also a café. See https://designmuseum.org for information.

Enter the park via the attractive 18th-century gilded **Wrought Iron Gates** ❷ bearing the Holland monogram, imported from Belgium by the 3rd Lord Holland and erected in 1836. Continue up the tarmac path, passing open sports fields and tennis courts on your left, with Holland Walk on your right. After around 400m you'll come to the Duchess of Bedford Walk entrance on your right and immediately ahead is the **Youth Hostel** ❸ (www.safestay.com/london-kensington-holland-park) in part of the remains of

Holland House ❹ (see box). The gloriously located hostel comprises three buildings, including the East Wing of the park's original Jacobean building, surrounding a private courtyard garden. Note the magnificent Portland stone **Gate Piers** ❺ in front of the terrace. Commissioned by Inigo Jones and made by Nicholas Stone in 1629, they were built as entrance gates to Holland House, but today act as a grand entrance to Opera Holland Park. The piers are composed of two Doric columns on pedestals, above which are carved griffins holding the Rich and Cope Arms. Opera Holland Park (www.operahollandpark.com) performs a summer season of open-air opera and theatre performances here

Holland House

Cope Castle (as it was then known) was built in 1605 for Sir Walter Cope (1553-1614), Chamberlain of the Exchequer to James I. Following his death it was inherited by his daughter Isabel, and was renamed Holland House after she married Henry Rich, 1st Earl of Holland in 1616 (he was executed in 1649 by Cromwell's puritans for his royalist activities). In the 19th century, Holland House became a hub of political and literary activity, visited by Disraeli and Lord Byron among others. It was severely damaged by bombs in 1940 and only the restored East Wing remains.

Milo of Croton

under a temporary canopy, with the remains of Holland House as a backdrop. Just past the gate piers you come to the park's **Café** 6 on your right. Inside are two of the park's many superb statues – **The Maid** 7 by Eric Gill and the **Sun God** 8, a 6ft (1.8m) relief of a male figure carved in limestone by Sir Jacob Epstein – brought indoors to protect them from inclement weather.

Enter the gardens through the arch to the left of the café and on the left is the original **Ice House** 9 , now used as an art gallery, which stages an annual programme of exhibitions from April to September. In front of the Ice House in the Iris Garden is the fountain **Sibirica** 10 by William Pye – based on a species of iris – installed in 1999. Behind the

fountain is the romantic **Belvedere Restaurant** 11 , housed in what was the summer ballroom. In front of the restaurant is a rose garden and to its left is the **Orangery** 12, a beautiful elegant building flooded with natural light that played host to Lord and Lady Holland's many receptions. Inside the Orangery are two 19th-century male nude bronzes, the **Wrestlers of Herculaneum** 13, copies of 4th-century statues from that ancient city (sculptor unknown).

Retrace your steps to the park map just beyond the garden entrance and go right (with the café on your right) passing the sculpture of the **Boy with Bear Cubs** 14 by John Macallan Swan. This delightful work depicts a naked boy standing on a tree stump; the boy is turning around to view one bear climbing up and in doing so tips his bowl of tit-bits to one side, where the second bear rears up for a snack. Continue along the path and turn left into the magnificent **Dutch Garden** 15, with vibrant flowerbeds enclosed by box hedges and numerous benches dedicated to loved ones. In the top right-hand corner of the garden is a Dutch **Wall Trough,** 16

Dutch Gardens

one of the house's original fountains, inscribed with the words: 'Earth would be less fair without trees to grace her valleys, Hide her scars, cast cool shade, In gardens here.' To the left are a number of sculptures including the limestone **Ancient Melancholy Man** 🄄 standing in a corner of the old brick wall – believed to date back to the 1500s – and the 19th-century bronze **Milo of Croton** 🄅 in the centre of the garden (inscription on the ground). Milo was a legendary Olympic athlete who hailed from Croton, a Greek settlement in southern Italy, in the 6th century BC. Further on, at the end of the garden – also called the Sundial Garden – is the **Armillary Sphere** 🄆 .

Armillary spheres are thought to have been developed by the Greek astronomer and philosopher Ptolemy in the 2nd century AD. They comprise a number of rings, known in Latin as *armillae*, representing the major circles on the celestial sphere, such as the horizon and the celestial equator. The Holland House sphere is a sundial. On the inside of the equator circle are etched the hours of the day and the time is shown by the shadow cast by the north pole/south pole axis rod (the gnomon), which points due north. Next to the Dutch Garden is a small garden with a giant chess set, followed by the **Napoleon Garden** 🄇 which takes its name from a bust of Napoleon by the Venetian sculptor Canova that once stood here. It's a discrete part of the park that's been used to

> ### Kyoto Garden
>
> One of the highlights of Holland Park is the beautiful Japanese Kyoto Garden, donated by Kyoto's Chamber of Commerce in 1991 to celebrate the Japan Festival held in London the following year. The garden is immaculately maintained and one of London's most tranquil and soul-soothing places, despite its resident pride of peacocks. It has a lovely pond stocked with colourful koi carp, with bobbing moorhens, stepping-stones and a 16ft (4.9m) waterfall. A stone path outlines the pond with a little bridge and viewing platform that crosses the pond at the base of the falls. The elegant plantings of Japanese shrubs and trees – including magnificent maples, cherry and magnolia – are at their best in spring and autumn, providing an ever-changing kaleidoscope of colour.

showcase contemporary sculpture since the 19th century.

From the Napoleon Garden, turn right back into the park and after a few minutes you

Boy with Bear Cubs

Walk 4

pass Sean Henry's **Walking Man** 21 (2000) on the right. At first glance 'he' appears to be a fellow walker, as the painted bronze figure is larger than life, like a three-dimensional painting. Straight ahead is the magical Japanese **Kyoto Garden** 22 (see box), with its waterfall and pond, entered through a wooden gate. There are actually two Japanese gardens close together. The Fukushima Garden was opened on 24 July 2012 to commemorate the support of the British people following the Fukushima nuclear disaster caused by the March 2011 tsunami. The garden is almost an empty space: a lawn on which a few rocks and a lantern are carefully placed, designed to evoke the feeling of emptiness left by the tsunami.

To the left of the garden is the **Ecology Centre** 23 – which offers environmental education programmes including nature walks, talks, programs for schools and outdoor activities for children – and the **Adventure Playground** 24 , which is equipped with swings, a giant see-saw, an aerial runway (zip wire) and a mini climbing wall.

Leave the Kyoto Garden on the left (opposite the waterfall), take the path to the right, and, on reaching the cross-path at the top of the rise, turn left down Lime Tree Avenue (planted by the 4th Lady Holland in 1876) and right at the junction just before its end. Walk to the end and enter a small garden in the northwest corner of the park, by the North Abbotsbury entrance, to see the imposing giant bronze sculpture **Tortoises with Triangle and Time** 25 , an imaginative sundial by Wendy Taylor. Retrace your steps back to the main path and take the uphill path to the left along the Chestnut Walk, a magical, peaceful wooded area. Near the top of the hill there are **Wildlife Enclosures** 26 on the left, where you may see cattle grazing. A little further on take the second of two paths on the right to view the superb George Frederick Watts' statue of **Henry Richard Vassal Fox, 3rd Baron Holland** 27 , who's seated on a throne-like chair in a pond in the woodland.

Kyoto Garden

Holland Park & Kyoto Garden

Turn left from the statue and continue along the path to the north of the park – passing a tree stump on the right at the crossroads – and exit the park via the **Sun Trap Entrance** 28 (near the Sun Terrace) into Holland

Food & Drink

6 **Holland Park Café:** A calm and tranquil oasis, the self-service café serves a range of home-made seasonal food, including take-away snacks and lunch boxes for kids (8.30am to 5.30pm, £).

11 **Belvedere Restaurant:** An elegant, if expensive, restaurant in a glorious location in the centre of the park, surrounded by flower gardens and lawns. The menu is classic French with a few British dishes, such as fish and chips and a Sunday roast (020-7602 1238, Mon-Fri noon-2.30pm, 6-10.30pm, Sun noon-3.30pm, ££).

29 **The Mitre:** Cosy pub on leafy Holland Park Avenue offering tasty food, cask ales and good wines (10am/noon-11pm/ midnight, £).

Park (road). Turn right, and at the end of the road is Holland Park Avenue. On the right-hand corner stands the incongruous statue of St Volodymyr, ruler of Ukraine 980-1015, erected near the Ukranian Embassy in 1988 to celebrate the establishment of Christianity in Ukraine 1,000 years earlier by St Volodymyr in 988.

Turn left on Holland Park Avenue and Holland Park tube station is around 100m up on the right. If you fancy a drink or a spot of lunch, there are a number of restaurants and pubs in Holland Park Avenue, including the cosy **Mitre** 29 at number 40.

1. Parliament Hill Lido
2. Parliament Hill Café
3. Stone of Free Speech
4. Highgate Men's Bathing Pond
5. Tumulus
6. Kenwood Ladies' Bathing Pond
7. Goodison Fountain
8. Kenwood House
9. Brew House Café
10. Monolith-Empyrean Sculpture
11. Flamme Sculpture
12. Two Piece Reclining Figure Sculpture
13. Stone Bridge
14. Hampstead Gate
15. Bird Bridge
16. Viaduct Bridge
17. Ice House
18. Vale of Health Pond
19. Pryor's Field
20. Mixed Bathing Pond
21. Parliament Hill
22. Southampton Arms Pub

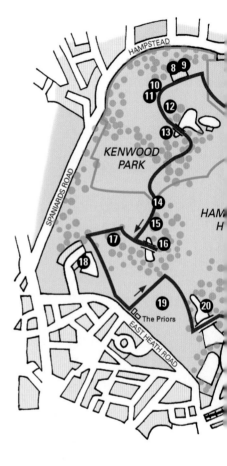

Places of Interest   Food & Drink

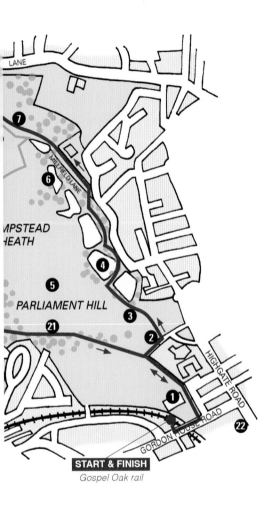

LANE

7

MILFIELD LANE

6

MPSTEAD
HEATH

4

5

PARLIAMENT HILL

3

21

2

1

HIGHGATE ROAD

22

GORDON HOUSE ROAD

START & FINISH
Gospel Oak rail

Hampstead Heath
& Kenwood Park

WALK 5

Walk 5

Distance: 5mi (8km)

Terrain: moderate, some steep hills

Duration: 2½ hours

Open: Unrestricted, Kenwood Park 8am to dusk

Start/End: Gospel Oak rail

Postcode: NW5 1LT

Hampstead Heath is an ancient swathe of green between Hampstead and Highgate, covering 790 acres (320ha), sitting astride one of the city's highest points (440ft/134m), yet just 6mi/10km from the centre of London. Rambling and hilly, it's one of London's most popular open spaces – attracting over 8 million visitors a year – encompassing grassland, woodland, gardens, ponds, playgrounds and a multitude of sports facilities. The Heath is an important haven for wildlife, including Muntjac deer, grass snakes, foxes, slow-worms, terrapins, frogs, rare insects and numerous bird species. Along its eastern perimeter is a chain of ponds – the Highgate Ponds – including two public swimming ponds, which are mirrored by the Hampstead Ponds on the western side.

The Heath was first recorded in 986 when Ethelred the Unready granted one of his servants five hides of land at 'Hemstede'. This same land was recorded in the *Domesday Book* of 1086 as being held by the monastery of St Peter's at Westminster Abbey, then known as the 'Manor of Hampstead'. Over time, plots of land were sold off for building, particularly in the early 19th century, although much of it remained common land. The main part was acquired by the Metropolitan Board of Works in 1871 for public use, while Parliament Hill was purchased in 1888 for £300,000 and added to the park and Kenwood House and its grounds in 1928. The surrounding areas of Golders Hill Park (1898) and Hill Garden (1960) are covered in Walk 6.

Since 1989, the Heath has been managed by the City of London Corporation and lies mostly within the borough of Camden, with the adjoining Hampstead Heath Extension and Golders Hill Park located in the

Hampstead Heath & Kenwood Park

borough of Barnet. It's a Local Nature Reserve and a Site of Metropolitan Importance, while part of Kenwood is a Site of Special Scientific Interest. There's unrestricted access to most of the Heath, with the exception of Kenwood Park.

Start Walking...

Leaving Gospel Oak rail station, turn left along Gordon House Road, passing under two bridges, and enter Hampstead Heath via the Gospel Oak entrance. Just to your left is **Parliament Hill Lido ❶**. Built in 1938 and Grade II-listed, it's the only stainless-steel lined outdoor pool in the country and opens from 7am each day. After around 300m, turn right at the crossroad passing the bandstand on your left and **Parliament Hill Café 2** – a good place for a caffeine fix. From the café follow the path on the right across Dukes Field with the **Stone of Free Speech ❸** to the left; this stone bollard is thought to have been the focus of religious and political meetings around 200 years ago. Continue straight ahead and pass between the first two Hampstead Ponds (see box) on your right: Highgate Pond No. 1 – also designated the 'dog pond' for four-legged bathers – and the **Highgate Men's Bathing Pond ❹**.

The ponds open from around 7am throughout the year (closing time varies – see www.cityoflondon.gov.uk > Hampstead Heath for times) and it costs £2 per day (£1 for concessions) to swim. When the City of London threatened to close the swimming ponds to save money some years ago, it caused such widespread outrage that they abandoned the plan (although they did introduce a fee). Look to the left (southwest) from the men's bathing pond to see the pine-topped **Tumulus ❺** where, according to local legend, Queen Boudicca (Boadicea) was buried after she and 10,000 Iceni warriors were defeated by the Romans at Battle Bridge (now King's Cross) in around 60AD.

Continue along the path to the right of the ponds to pass the Model Boating Pond, the

Hampstead Ponds

Hampstead Ponds is a generic term often used for the various ponds on the west and east sides of Hampstead Heath. The ponds are fed by the headwater springs of the River Fleet, which flows underground into the Thames near Blackfriars Bridge. They were originally dug in the 17th and 18th centuries as reservoirs to meet London's growing demand for water. Out of the 30 or so ponds on the Heath, three are designated swimming ponds, one for men, one for women and one for mixed bathing. Water birds such as herons, great crested grebes and cormorants can also be seen here – if you're lucky you may even catch a glimpse of a kingfisher.

Bird Sanctuary Pond and the **Kenwood Ladies' Bathing Pond** ❻. The latter is restricted to women and girls aged over 8. Women have swum here since the '20s and, apart from an aerator added to the water to prevent the pond icing over in winter, very little has changed since. It's a beautiful, serene and secluded spot, where you can swim with kingfishers and herons. The final pond on this path is the Stock Pond, fed by Highgate Brook and close to the Kenwood Estate.

Just past the Stock Pond is the **Goodison Fountain** ❼, whose water is free flowing and rich in iron. It was erected in 1929 in memory of Henry Goodison who founded the Kenwood Preservation Society to save Kenwood House and the surrounding land for the public. In summer, meadow brown and orange tip butterflies and swifts can be seen in the meadow beyond, while in winter flocks of fieldfares and redwings arrive from Scandinavia. The path follows the boundary fence of Kenwood Estate on the left, where you enter the estate via the Millfield

> **Kenwood House**
>
> An elegant villa built in the 17th century, it was owned for over 200 years by the family of William Murray, the 1st Earl of Mansfield (1705-1793). The house was remodelled between 1764 and 1773 by Robert Adam, who transformed the original brick house into a majestic neoclassical villa. Brewing magnate Edward Cecil Guinness, first Earl of Iveagh (1847-1927), purchased Kenwood House and Estate in 1925. He bequeathed both to the nation, along with most of his stunning collection of old masters (known as the Iveagh Bequest), which includes something to suit every taste, from Rembrandt to Turner, Gainsborough to Vermeer. The house and collection are well worth a visit (open daily 10am-5pm, 4pm in winter).

Gate – straight ahead is **Kenwood House** ❽ (see box).

Kenwood Estate encompasses 112 acres (45ha) of landscaped parkland enclosing Kenwood House (Grade II* listed), managed by English Heritage; entrance to the estate and house is free. In contrast to the natural heathland, the park around Kenwood House was created by the eminent English landscape gardener Humphry Repton (1752-1818), and was designed to be seen

Kenwood House

Hampstead Heath & Kenwood Park

② **Parliament Hill Café:**
Popular café offering
a wide range of food,
including jacket potatoes,
sandwiches, full English
breakfast, ice cream and
cakes (9am-6pm, £).

⑨ **Brew House Café:**
Situated in Kenwood
House, this delightful
café offers a good choice
of tasty food, including
veggie and children's
options, while in summer
there's a stand serving ice
cream and Pimm's (9am-
4/6pm, £).

㉒ **The Southampton Arms:**
A spruced-up traditional
boozer ('Ale & Cider
House') on Highgate Road
near Hampstead Heath's
Gospel Oak entrance,
offering a wide range of
cask ales (noon-10.30pm/
midnight, £).

spot for an alfresco drink or lunch
on the terrace on a fine day.

Kenwood House interior

Although bordered on three
sides by Hampstead Heath,
Kenwood was maintained as a
designed landscape until the '50s
with a different character from
the Heath. One third of the estate
(Ken Wood and North Wood) is
semi-natural ancient woodland
with a vast rhododendron
collection. It's also home to many
birds and insects and the largest
pipistrelle bat roost in London.
Highlights include the walled
garden with its kidney-shaped
butterfly bed and ivy arch, leading
to a raised terrace with stunning
views over the lakes. The inner
and outer circuit routes take you
around lawns, over bridges and
through woods, following the
original walks laid out by Repton.
The gardens near the house
contain sculptures by Barbara

from a planned circuit walk that
provides a series of evocative
views, contrasts and 'surprises'.
If you have the time it's well
worth exploring, with meandering
paths, ancient woodland, beautiful
sculptures and much more. The
Brew House Café ⑨ is a lovely

Hampstead Heath has had its own
dedicated police presence since 1889
and its own constabulary since 1992,
consisting of 13 constables (and six
police dogs), which is responsible for
patrolling the Heath and enforcing its
byelaws.

Walk 5

Hepworth, Henry Moore and Reg Butler, among others.

Once you've had your fill of coffee, cakes and culture, follow Lime Avenue path from Kenwood House with the flower garden on your right. At the end of the garden take a small detour to the right to see Barbara Hepworth's sculpture **Monolith-Empyrean** ⑩ ('heavenly stone'), a modern limestone work created in 1953. Back on Lime Avenue, just as the path curves round to the left there's a short path to the right, where you can see **Flamme** ⑪, a monumental stone statue by French sculptor Eugène Dodeigne (1983). Lime Avenue also hosts the huge Henry Moore bronze, **Two Piece Reclining Figure No. 5** ⑫, sculpted in 1963-4, before you head downhill to the **Stone Bridge** ⑬ over Wood Pond in the centre of the estate. Beyond this is the Thousand Pound Pond – possibly given this name after Lord Mansfield sold some land here in 1922 for £1,000 per acre – and the white Sham Bridge (which is just a façade built 1755-57). You have walked in a wide semi-circle – looking back there's a wonderful view of Kenwood House.

After crossing the Stone Bridge, turn sharp right into the woods, following the fence which overlooks West Meadow valley on your right. Continue along a winding path – surrounded by soaring ancient trees and birdsong – through the woods to **Hampstead Gate** ⑭ and back onto Hampstead Heath. From the gate take the path downhill on the left, then go left again around a tight bend and take the next (narrow) path on the right at the junction through the trees, which takes you to **Bird Bridge** ⑮. Cross and turn left at the T-junction of the two main paths ahead and you soon arrive at the **Viaduct Bridge** ⑯ from where there are more panoramic views.

Retrace your steps to the T-junction and turn left onto the Vale of Health estate road. Sir Thomas Maryon Wilson, who had

Parliament Hill

Parliament Hill – formerly known as Traitors' Hill – is said to get its name from its designation by Parliamentary forces during the Civil War as a defence point for London. At the summit there's a viewpoint indicator that identifies buildings in the wide panorama over central London, six miles (10km) to the south. Many landmarks can be seen from its summit including Canary Wharf, the Gherkin, the Shard, the London Eye and St Paul's Cathedral. You can also make out the Houses of Parliament, although they have become rather obscured by surrounding buildings.

manorial rights over this part of the Heath, constructed the road in 1845; he had a grand plan to build on the Heath, which was thwarted by local protests. A hundred metres further on you arrive at the **Ice House** 🟤 on your left, a small building with a conical roof used to store ice before the days of modern refrigeration.

Take a left just past the Ice House south towards the **Vale of Health Pond** 🟤, a favourite fishing area. The curved north-eastern bank follows the enclosed, tree-lined footpath providing a natural edge to the pond with openings at either corner. The pond attracts a range of bird life, including swans. Straight ahead from the pond are two large blocks of flats called The Pryors, where you turn left onto Lime Avenue skirting **Pryor's Field** 🟤, and

right at the next intersection. This will take you to the three Hampstead Ponds, the first of which (on the left) is the **Mixed Bathing Pond** 🟤.

Cross the bridge with the bathing pond on your left and continue uphill along this path – keeping to the right and crossing over two paths – and ascend to the summit of **Parliament Hill** 🟤 (see box), which is one of the highest points on Hampstead Heath. Also known as Kite Hill, it's a popular spot for kite flyers.

From Parliament Hill, head downhill to the bandstand and Lido, returning to Gospel Oak rail station the way you came. If you fancy a drink, the **Southampton Arms** 🟤 offers a wide choice of cask ales and is a few minutes' walk away in Highgate Road.

Hampstead Heath

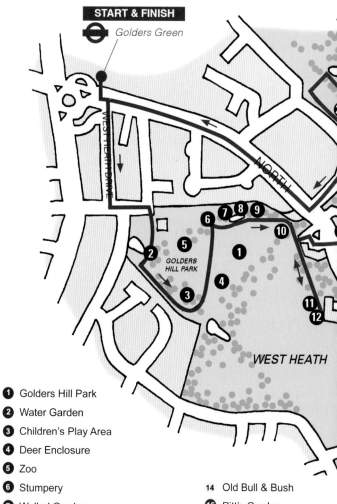

START & FINISH
Golders Green

GOLDERS
HILL PARK

WEST HEATH

1. Golders Hill Park
2. Water Garden
3. Children's Play Area
4. Deer Enclosure
5. Zoo
6. Stumpery
7. Walled Garden
8. Boy with Fish Fountain
9. Golders Hill Girl Sculpture
10. Golders Hill Park Refreshment House
11. Hill Garden
12. Pergola
13. Inverforth House

14. Old Bull & Bush
15. Pitt's Garden
16. Sandy Heath
17. Sandy Heath Ponds
18. Spaniards Inn
19. Ikins Corner
20. Heath Extension
21. Seven Sisters Ponds

● Places of Interest   ○ Food & Drink

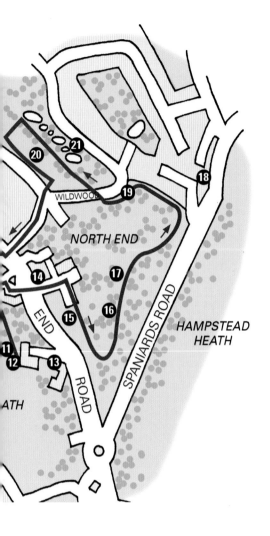

WILDWOOD

NORTH END

END

ROAD

SPANIARDS ROAD

HAMPSTEAD HEATH

ATH

20 **21** **19** **18** **14** **17** **15** **16** **11** **12** **13**

Golders Hill Park & Hill Garden

Distance: 4½mi (7¼km)

Terrain: moderate, hilly in places

Duration: 2-2½ hours

Open: 7.30/8.30am to dusk

Start/End: Golders Green tube

Postcode: NW3 7ES

GOLDERS HILL PARK & HILL GARDEN

Opened in 1898, Golders Hill Park is a formal park adjoining the western part of Hampstead Heath. It has been managed as a separate part of the heath by the City of London since 1989 and, unlike most of the rest of the heath, it's closed at night. The site was formerly occupied by Golders Hill House, which was built in the 1760s by Charles Dingley but destroyed during World War Two.

The main characteristics of the park are a large expanse of grass (ideal for games and sports) dotted with specimen trees, a beautiful formal English flower garden, a Mediterranean garden, a walled garden, and a water garden with a number of ponds. The ponds are stocked with marsh and water plants and are home to a large number of water birds, including black and white swans. Paths wind their way around the park, criss-crossing and meandering beneath trees, past water features and through secret vales. The park also contains a zoo, butterfly house, deer enclosure, café, bandstand and children's play area, and offers a variety of sports and leisure facilities, including tennis courts, a croquet lawn, golf practice nets and a putting green.

In the eastern section of the park, the charming Hill Garden and its exquisite pergola are among the hidden delights of Hampstead Heath. The formal Arts and Crafts garden was created between 1906 and 1925 by celebrated landscape architect Thomas Mawson (1861-1933), and is situated at the rear of Inverforth House. The area was restored and opened to the public in 1963 as the Hill Garden, and in 1995 the City of London Corporation restored the wild decadence of the unique pergola and laid out further formal gardens to the west. It's a beautifully manicured slice of paradise, affording panoramic views over London.

Golders Hill Park & Hill Garden

Start Walking…

From Golders Green tube station, cross over North End Road, turn left and take the second right down West Heath Avenue. After around 400m you arrive at the entrance to **Golders Hill Park** ❶. Follow the path around the tennis courts to the Swan Pond and the **Water Garden** ❷, cross over a small humpback bridge between the first two ponds and follow the path round to the **Children's Play Area.** ❸ The natural ponds are part of a chain that traverses Hampstead Heath. Follow the path straight ahead, passing the (fallow) **Deer Enclosure** ❹, to the **Zoo** ❺ (see box) in the middle of the park, which is – surprise, surprise – popular with kids.

> ### NOTE
> Unlike most of Hampstead Heath, dogs must be kept on a lead in the park and they aren't permitted at all in the Hill Garden.

Heading north past the zoo, take the path to the right (leading to the café), with the broad expanse of lawn on your right, and you'll pass the **Stumpery** ❻ on your left. An interesting feature of the park, this is an artistically arranged collection of tree stumps, with ferns and woodland plants which develop the right conditions for mosses and lichens to flourish. It provides nesting and feeding sites for insects and birds, and plenty of secluded hollows for small mammals such as hedgehogs. Just past the Stumpery is the Lily Pond, and behind that a beautiful

> ### Zoo
> Golders Hill Park is home to a free zoo – actually more a series of animal enclosures or large cages – with a collection of rare and exotic birds (beautiful egrets!) and mammals, such as laughing kookaburras, ring-tailed lemurs and ring-tailed coatis.

Walled Garden ❼ containing many exotic trees and shrubs, and a pond with a charming fountain titled **Boy with Fish** ❽. The small butterfly house (2-4pm, April to October) nearby is free of charge and allows you to see many British and tropical species close up, and to study the life cycle of these fascinating insects.

Golders Hill Girl

Just past the Lily Pond is the **Golders Hill Girl** ❾, a lovely bronze by Patricia Finch (1991) of a reclining girl with her flip-flops by her side. Opposite, on the far side of the huge expanse of lawn, is the bandstand, where there's live music on Sunday afternoons in summer. A few hundred metres past the walled garden you come to the café (and toilets), located just inside the eastern entrance to the park from North End Road.

Walk 6

Pergola

The brainchild of Lord Leverhulme, the owner of Inverforth House in the early 1900s, the pergola (Grade II listed) was restored in the early '90s. It's a wonderful example of faded grandeur and is one of London's hidden treasures. It's essentially a raised zigzagging walkway set amidst some wonderfully dramatic gardens, offering stunning views over the heath. In late spring and early summer it's festooned with fragrant flowers, including jasmine, buddleia, sage, honeysuckle, vines, clematis, kiwi, potato vine, lavender and wisteria. If you visit during the early evening you may even see roosting long-eared bats.

Rather grandly titled the **Golders Hill Park Refreshment House** 10 , it's been managed for over 40 years by Italian Alberto Pazienti and his family, and offers good food and coffee, not to mention their famous home-made ice cream (try the mint and chocolate).

From the café take the path directly opposite, cross over Sandy Road (there's a mansion house on the left) and climb a flight of rustic stairs. At the top, take the left-hand fork past a huge dead tree and follow the meandering path to the end. The entrance to **Hill Garden** 11 – one of the highlights of the walk – is directly opposite. The beautiful

and tranquil garden (open 8.30am to dusk) is one of London's best-kept secrets, along with its magnificent **Pergola** 12 (see box).

The history of the Pergola dates back to 1904, when Lord Leverhulme, a wealthy philanthropist and lover of landscape gardening who made his fortune from Sunlight soap, purchased a large town house called The Hill. He quickly expanded his estate by acquiring surrounding land, and with this newfound space he decided to build a legacy: the Pergola. He envisaged it as the perfect setting for extravagant Edwardian garden parties, and a place where family and friends could spend long summer evenings enjoying the spectacular gardens.

To turn his idea into reality Lord Leverhulme enlisted the help of Thomas Mawson, the world-famous landscape architect, and construction began in 1905. To raise the gardens required an extraordinary amount of material, but fortunately for Mawson the nearby Hampstead extension of the Northern underground line provided the solution. Instead of bringing in material from further afield (at huge cost), a deal was

struck to shuttle the spoil from the underground extension just a few hundred metres to The Hill. Progress was quick, and the Pergola was finished a year later. Over subsequent years, Lord Leverhulme was able to expand his estate further, allowing for a further extension of the Pergola in 1911 and again in 1925. It's now some 800ft (244m) in length, as long as the Canary Wharf Tower is tall.

Hill Garden is a fine example of its era and has a unique atmosphere of mellowed classicism. It's a fascinating place to explore with many twists and turns that lead to the discovery of enchanting nooks and crannies. In contrast to the luxuriant abandon of the vegetation on the Pergola, the garden is a beautifully maintained oasis in this hidden corner of north London. The Pergola Walk links the formal gardens of the main house and the more gentle sloping lawns of the lower garden, with a lovely lily pond, mature trees and shrubs – and lots of benches from which to admire your surroundings.

Adjoining Hill Garden is splendid **Inverforth House** ⑬,

Hill Garden

formerly named The Hill, built in 1895 and renamed when it was sold on Lord Leverhulme's death in 1925 to Andrew Weir, 1st Baron Inverforth. The house is fenced off from the Pergola, but you can admire it from afar. From Hill Garden head back towards the café in Golders Hill Park and cross over North End Way into North End, past the **Old Bull & Bush** 14 pub. A little way past the pub turn right into North End Avenue, where, just off the beaten track, is **Pitt's Garden** ⑮. Here, William Pitt the Elder (1708-1778), Prime Minister 1766-1768 and later 1st Earl of Chatham, shut himself away for months in 1767 after suffering a nervous breakdown while serving as Prime Minister. The house was demolished in 1952, and all that remains of

Gibbet Elms

The infamous 'Gibbet Elms' once stood close to Hill Garden, where the bodies of highwaymen were hung in a suspended iron framework as a warning to others. According to local legend, Dick Turpin was active on the heath and is thought to have used the Spaniards Inn (to the northeast of the garden) – where his father was the landlord – as a hideout.

Walk 6

the estate is the large walled garden, now part of the heath, and a spectacular wilderness with a ruined classical archway. It contains areas of recently planted heather, the heath's signature plant.

This area is known as **Sandy Heath** **16**, a dramatic lunar-like landscape with steep slopes, sudden hollows and undulations, the result of clay, sand and gravel extraction in the 1860s for making bricks and laying railways. The once despoiled terrain has been colonised by birch, beech and oak trees which provide a habitat for nesting birds such as long-tailed tits.

From Pitt's Garden, follow the path in a loop across Sandy Heath to the right of **Sandy Heath Ponds** **17** (aka the Iron Pan Ponds), an interconnected series of ponds in the middle of the heath and along Sandy Road. At the end of the path, across Spaniards

Road, is Mount Tyndal (a luxury apartment building), while further along is the **Spaniards Inn** **18** public house, allegedly a haunt of the notorious highwayman Dick Turpin, with an 18th-century Toll Gate House (Spaniards Gate) opposite. Follow the path to the left around the edge of the heath until you come to **Ikins Corner** **19** – which marks the border between the heath proper and the **Heath Extension** **20** – an open space created out of farmland. Its origins can still be seen in the old field boundaries, hedgerows and trees, while the northern section is mainly given over to sports fields.

Follow the path to the right with a hedgerow to the left, a remnant of the ancient Wylde Wood, with oaks and hornbeams interspersed with hazel, hawthorn and elder. To your right are the **Seven Sisters Ponds** **21** that feed into Brent Reservoir. In summer a variety of damselflies and dragonflies,

including the azure blue damselfly and the common darter dragonfly, can be seen patrolling the area. At the end of the ponds take a left and make your way back to the heath along the western edge of the extension, taking Hampstead Way and bearing right where it joins Wildwood Road, to head back towards Golders Hill Park Refreshment House. If you fancy a pint after your exertions,

Hampstead Heath Extension

Food & Drink

⑩ Golders Hill Park Refreshment House: Just inside the North End Road entrance to Golders Hill Park, the café offers good food and coffee and a famous range of sumptuous ice cream (9am-6pm, £).

⑭ The Old Bull & Bush: Located opposite Golders Hill Park, the Old B&B is a large gastropub with a modern European menu, cosy bar and outdoor terrace (11am-10.30/11pm, £).

⑱ The Spaniards Inn: Historic, atmospheric hostelry dating from 1585 with associations with Dickens, Keats and Bram Stoker. Good food and ales and huge beer garden.

you may like to stop off at the **Old Bull & Bush 14**, just a few minutes away along North End Way.

This is the end of the walk. From the café (or pub), simply retrace your steps through the park (or along North End Road) back to Golders Green tube station.

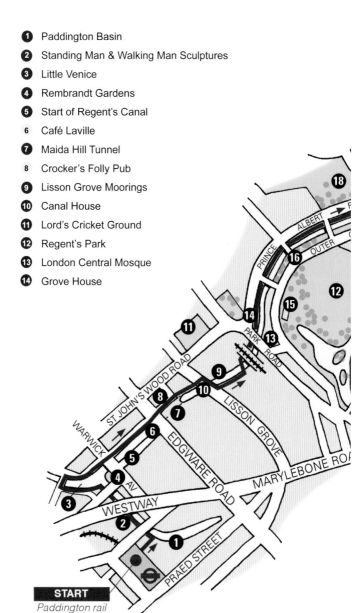

1. Paddington Basin
2. Standing Man & Walking Man Sculptures
3. Little Venice
4. Rembrandt Gardens
5. Start of Regent's Canal
6. Café Laville
7. Maida Hill Tunnel
8. Crocker's Folly Pub
9. Lisson Grove Moorings
10. Canal House
11. Lord's Cricket Ground
12. Regent's Park
13. London Central Mosque
14. Grove House

START
Paddington rail

Places of Interest   Food & Drink

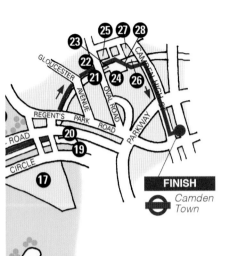

FINISH
Camden Town

- **15** Winfield House
- **16** Macclesfield Bridge
- **17** London Zoo
- **18** Primrose Hill
- **19** Cumberland Basin
- **20** Feng Shang Princess
- **21** The Pirate Castle
- **22** Pumping Station
- **23** Banksy Artwork
- **24** Gilbey's Gin Warehouse
- **25** The Interchange Warehouse
- **26** Camden Lock
- 27 Camden Market
- **28** The Turnover Bridge

WALK 7

Regent's Canal

Distance: 3mi (5km)

Terrain: easy, some steps

Duration: 1½ hours

Open: unrestricted

Start: Paddington tube/rail

End: Camden Town tube

Postcode: W2 1HB

REGENT'S CANAL

The Regent's Canal – opened in 1820 and named after the Prince Regent (later George IV) – links the Paddington arm of the Grand Junction Canal with the River Thames at Limehouse in East London, a distance of 8.6mi (13.8km). Today it forms part of the Jubilee Greenway, a 37-mile (60km) route around north London. The section we have chosen for this walk runs from Little Venice in Maida Vale to Camden Town via Lord's Cricket Ground, Regent's Park and London Zoo.

It's one of the most tranquil sections of the Jubilee Greenway, packed with interest, changing character from one bridge to the next, and leading the walker, cyclist or traveller by boat from the smart residential area of Little Venice to bustling Camden Market. Regent's Canal offers one of the most idyllic walks in London, particularly on a sunny day when the barges and boats are active, and the lovely Regency villas are sparkling in the sunshine.

Any city canal offers an interesting warts-and-all stroll and the Regent's Canal is no exception, flowing through a series of contrasting landscapes, from Regency splendour to 19th-century industrial bleakness to seemingly open countryside, with a few surprises along the way. It offers a rare glimpse behind the scenes of the city, catching it with its guard down.

Before setting out, take some time to explore Little Venice, one of the city's most serene backwaters, and allow an hour or two at the end to wander around fascinating Camden Market – and hopefully pick up a bargain. Like all the walks in this book, you can, of course, reverse the direction – and this walk has the added bonus of allowing you to return to your starting point by waterbus.

Start Walking…

Leave Paddington Station by the exit for **Paddington Basin** ❶, the terminus of the Paddington arm of the Grand Junction Canal (later the Grand Union Canal). Take the path left along the basin, which goes under Bishop's Bridge Road and the Westway, where you pass **Standing Man & Walking Man** ❷, two slightly unnerving life-like statues by Sean Henry. The basin leads to **Little Venice** ❸ (see box) and adjoins Browning's Pool – where the Regent's and Grand Junction Canals meet. The pool and the island at its centre are both named in honour of the poet Robert Browning, who lived near here.

One of London's most exclusive residential areas, Little Venice is an unexpected haven of calm and beauty. The canal is lined with weeping willows and flanked by graceful, stuccoed Regency mansions, many designed by noted architect John Nash. Houseboats painted in bright

> ### Little Venice
>
> A tranquil throwback to a time when London was a collection of villages, the name Little Venice is used rather loosely, but technically speaking it's the area where the westernmost point of the Regent's Canal meets the Grand Union Canal and the Paddington Basin. Nowadays it's used in a wider context to describe an area of around a square mile in Maida Vale, although the name didn't come into general use until after World War Two. The myth persists that the term was coined by the poet Robert Browning (1812-1889), who compared the area, around what was then 'The Broadwater', with Venice in Italy. His beloved wife Elizabeth Barrett died in Italy in 1861, and Browning returned to London where he lived in a house on Warwick Crescent, overlooking the canal, until 1887. He died two years later – in Venice, Italy – and his body is interred in Poet's Corner in Westminster Abbey.

red, dark green and navy blue dot the canal, some with window boxes bursting with flowers, others adorned with elaborate nameplates, while ducks, geese and swans drift languidly by.

Take the path clockwise around Browning's Pool, passing the Waterside Café (housed on a narrowboat), and cross over the blue footbridge on the west side of the pool, where you pass the Puppet Theatre Barge. Tranquil **Rembrandt Gardens** ❹ run along the eastern side of Browning's Pool, offering panoramic views over Little Venice. Follow the towpath – which runs parallel to Blomfield Road – under Warwick Avenue Bridge and along the **Regent's Canal** ❺, which starts here. This

stretch of canal is lined on both sides by grand Regency-style terraces.

Soon after the bridge (just past the lock keeper's house), the towpath is closed by a metal gate and walkers are diverted up steps to Blomfield Road. The next 300m or so of the towpath belongs exclusively to the occupants of the private

Café Laville

moored narrowboats. Follow the narrow pavement, squeezing past plane trees, and just beyond the moorings by Maida Hill Tunnel you come to **Café Laville** 6 , a splendid Italian café bridging the canal. On a sunny day there are few better places to enjoy a coffee than the terrace overlooking the canal.

The café sits atop the entrance to the **Maida Hill Tunnel** 7 – 440m in length – and as there's no way through by foot you must go over ground, crossing busy Edgware Road to Aberdeen

> ### Crocker's Folly
>
> This hostelry dates from the 1890s when one Frank Crocker built a hotel to cash in on trade from the planned nearby terminus of the Great Central Railway. No expense was spared, but unfortunately the railway's route was changed, the hotel was unsuccessful, and the name was changed to Crocker's Folly. Today, the beautifully restored (Grade II listed) building is one of London's most stunning pubs (don't miss the glorious Marble Room).

Place. Look for number 32 on the left which has a blue plaque to Guy Gibson, who led the famous Dambusters raid on the Ruhr valley in May 1943. A few hundred metres further (on the left) is the **Crocker's Folly** 8 pub (see box). The road swings left into Cunningham Place, but there's an alleyway on the right – tucked between a brick wall and an electricity substation – which leads you back to the canal and the footpath which runs alongside it (the towpath appears to be permanently closed here). Follow the path along the edge of the canal (not the towpath) to Lisson Grove.

Cross the bridge at Lisson Grove (Eyre's Tunnel) over the canal and rejoin the (southern) towpath opposite Frampton

Lisson Grove Moorings

Street, which offers expansive views of the moored narrowboats at **LIsson Grove Moorings** (9); there are paths both north and south of the canal here, although the northern path is sometimes closed. Over the tunnel under Lisson Grove is **Canal House** (10) at No 120, built in 1906 for the manager of Regent's Canal; it's the only property in London that forms a bridge over a canal.

To the north of the canal is **Lord's Cricket Ground** (11), home of the Marylebone Cricket Club (MCC), the guardian of the laws of

London Centra Mosque

the game. The original ground was in the path of the proposed canal and the MCC were paid £4,000 to move it some 500m northwest; the 'new' ground opened in 1814. After Lisson Grove moorings you cross back to the north side of the canal via a footbridge before passing under a cluster of road and rail bridges. The last bridge (Park Road) opens out onto a tranquil vista with grand mansions lining the opposite side of the canal alongside **Regent's Park** (12) (see **Walk 3**), their gardens and weeping willows tumbling down to the water.

The mansions are heralded by the prominent minaret and dome of the vast **London Central Mosque** (13), set back

Food & Drink

(6) **Café Laville:** Splendid Italian café overlooking the canal (9.30/10am-10/10.30pm, £).

(8) **Crocker's Folly:** A stunning pub, serving delicious Lebanese cuisine (noon-11/11.30pm, £).

(27) **Camden Market:** The market offers dozens of food and drink options. Some of our favourites include the Lantana Camden for first-rate coffee and cakes, Yumchaa for a superb cup of tea and the Lockside Bar & Kitchen, a hip canalside bar with a rooftop terrace, if you fancy something stronger.

from the canal, which opened in 1977 and can accommodate 4,500 worshippers. Just past the mosque on the left side of the towpath is the imposing **Grove House** (14), HQ of the Nuffield Foundation from 1952 to 1986. It was designed by Decimus Burton and completed in 1824, and the gardens which run alongside the canal are amongst the largest in London. A little further on, set back behind the villas flanking the canal on the right, is **Winfield House** 15 , official residence of the US Ambassador since 1955. It was built in 1937 for Barbara Hutton, heiress to the Woolworth store empire, who 'sold' it to the US government after World War Two for $1.

Macclesfield Bridge

The canal arcs around the northern edge of Regent's Park, going under Chalbert Street footbridge – which also doubles as an aqueduct carrying the Tyburn River – before reaching **Macclesfield Bridge** 16 . This bridge is more commonly referred to by its nickname 'Blow Up Bridge', which dates from an incident in 1874 when a boat carrying a cargo of gunpowder bound for the Midlands exploded here, killing three of the crew and demolishing the bridge and several houses. The canal was repaired and back in use within five days.

A few hundred metres past Macclesfield Bridge is **London Zoo** 17 (see box), which straddles both sides of the canal, with Lord Snowdon's Aviary looming large over the north bank. You can

access the zoo via the Broad Walk path, which intersects with the towpath just after the zoo. To the north, beyond the aviary, is **Primrose Hill** 18 (62 acres/25ha), ostensibly part of Regent's Park. It's one of London's most scenic spots and celebrated for its grassy slopes, stunning views and roll-call of famous residents.

A short way past London Zoo, just after St Mark's Bridge, the canal opens into **Cumberland Basin** 19 , with its moored narrowboats and a floating Chinese restaurant, **Feng Shang Princess** 20 . The basin is all that remains of the 800m Cumberland Arm or Spur, which was built to serve Cumberland Market (the market closed in the '30s, and the basin was dammed off in 1938). Here the canal turns to the left and goes under a number of low road and rail bridges, where gardens flow down to the water's edge. Just before the Oval Road bridge, on the south side of the canal, is

London Zoo

Opened in 1828, London Zoo (also called Regent's Zoo) is the world's oldest zoo. It didn't admit the public until 1847 but is now one of London's premier attractions. It houses one of the largest collections of animals in the world (some 700 species), from giraffes to gorillas, although in recent years some larger animals, such as elephants and rhinos, have been moved to the zoo's sister site at Whipsnade in Bedfordshire.

The Pirate Castle ㉑ , a water-based charity providing canoeing, kayaking and canal boating for disadvantaged young people. Opposite the castle is a **Pumping Station** ㉒ , built in the same style, which pumps water to cool the high-tension electricity cables that run beneath the towpath. Before leaving here take a few minutes to admire the **Banksy Artwork** ㉓ close to the bridge.

Emerging from under the Oval Road bridge, on the south side is the former **Gilbey's Gin Warehouse** ㉔ , built in 1894 and now an apartment building. A little further on, just before you reach Camden Lock, is the **Interchange Warehouse** ㉕ – built in 1905 and now offices – where the towpath incorporates a humpback back bridge (the Interchange basin is known locally as Dead Dog Hole). This was the barge entrance to the warehouse where goods were transferred between canal, rail and road. A few paces on you reach **Camden Lock** ㉖ , one of the busiest sites on the canal, particularly at weekends when tourists and Londoners flock to **Camden Market** 27 (see box).

Camden Lock marks the end of this walk. To reach Camden Town tube station, cross over the **Turnover Bridge** ㉘ (aka Roving Bridge)**,** which was created so that barge horses could cross the canal while towing. Originally this was the only point on the canal, heading east, where the towpath was on the right-hand side. Once over the bridge, follow the canal to Camden High Street and turn right; Camden Town tube station is a few hundred metres up on the left. Alternatively, if you're returning to Little Venice, you can take the 45-minute waterbus service from Camden Lock.

Camden Market

Created as an arts and crafts market in the '70s, Camden Market (or Camden Lock) is one of the city's coolest destinations. It's comprised of six adjoining markets and at weekends attracts up to 150,000 bargain hunters.

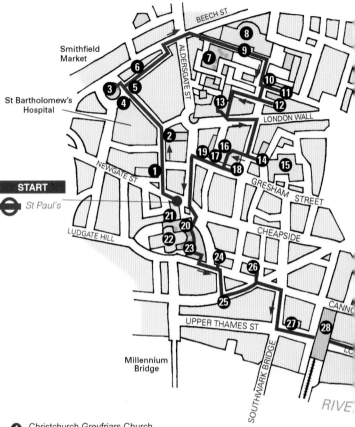

Smithfield Market

St Bartholomew's Hospital

BEECH ST

ALDERSGATE ST

LONDON WALL

NEWGATE ST

START

St Paul's

GRESHAM STREET

LUDGATE HILL

CHEAPSIDE

UPPER THAMES ST

CANNON

Millennium Bridge

SOUTHWARK BRIDGE

RIVER

1 Christchurch Greyfriars Church Garden

2 Postman's Park

3 West Smithfield Rotunda Garden

4 Memorial to the Peasants' Revolt of 1381

5 St Bartholomew the Great

6 Cloth Fair

7 The Barbican Estate

8 Barbican Centre

9 Lakeside Terrace

10 St Giles Cripplegate

11 Salters' Hall & Garden

12 St Alphage Garden

13 Barber-Surgeons' Hall Gardens

14 St Mary Aldermanbury Garden

15 Guildhall

16 St Mary Staining Churchyard

17 St John Zachary Garden

18 The Three Printers Sculpture

19 St Anne & St Agnes Church

20 St Paul's Churchyard Garden

21 The Paternoster Pub

22 St Paul's Cathedral

Places of Interest   Food & Drink

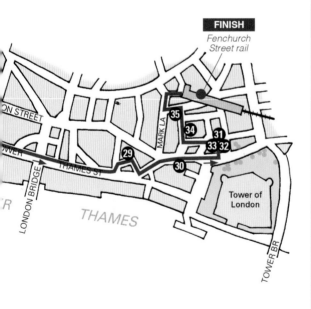

WALK 8

City of London
Parks & Gardens

Walk 8

Distance: 4½mi (7¼km)

Terrain: easy, some hills and stairs

Duration: 2-2½ hours

Open: unrestricted or Mon-Fri 9am-5pm

Start: St Paul's tube

End: Fenchurch Street rail

Postcode: EC2V 6AA

The history of London stretches back some 2,000 years, during which time it has experienced plagues and invasions, devastating fires, civil war, aerial bombardment, terrorist attacks and widespread rioting. The first stones of the city were laid by the all-conquering Romans, who founded Londinium around 50AD, but when they left Britain in 410AD it went into rapid decline. In the following centuries, Britain was invaded by a succession of tribes –Angles, Saxons and Jutes and, later, Vikings – but it wasn't until 1066, when the Normans invaded from France and William the Conqueror took the British crown that London came back on the map.

In medieval times the City of London constituted virtually the whole of London; nowadays it's a tiny geographical part of Greater London, although still know as the City of London. The City's small scale is reflected in its nickname 'The Square Mile', although it actually covers slightly more. Its resident population is tiny – around 8,000 – although this is swelled by some 400,000 daily commuters, many of whom work in the UK's financial services industry (aka 'the City'), and over 10 million annual visitors.

Although it has no large parks, the City of London has some 200 small, 'secret' spaces; many have sprung up in the ruins of old churches and cemeteries, while others have been created by the Guilds that once dominated the City's trades. Each has its own particular charms and attractions, and they provide an oasis for people and wildlife in one of the world's busiest metropolises. Most are open during normal business hours, but do check in advance if there's a particular garden you want to see.

Start Walking…

From St Paul's tube station, take exit 2 and cross Newgate Street at the traffic lights, continue to your left and cross King Edward Street to reach **Christchurch Greyfriars Church Garden ❶**. This enchanting small garden was created on the remains of a ruined Wren church, where several incarnations of Christchurch Greyfriars have stood since 1306; the last was severely damaged in the Blitz and never rebuilt, although the tower still stands. Leaving the garden, turn left along King Edward Street to **Postman's Park ❷** (see box) on the right-hand side; its name reflects its popularity with workers from the old Post Office HQ.

St Bartholomew the Great

Continue up King Edward Street into Little Britain and follow it around to the left, keeping to the side of St Bart's Hospital; where it turns right into Bartholomew Close, take a left along an alleyway to reach **West Smithfield Rotunda Garden ❸**, opposite Smithfield Market. This pretty and peaceful circular garden has a gruesome history. For over 400 years it was a place of public execution, where heretics, rebels and criminals were burnt, beheaded or boiled! In 1305, Scottish hero William Wallace was dragged to Smithfield behind a horse to be hung, drawn and quartered, and over 200 Protestants were burnt at the stake here during the reign of Queen 'Bloody' Mary. On the wall facing the garden near the exit from Little Britain is a **Memorial to the Peasants' Revolt of 1381 ❹**, a protest by thousands

---

Postman's Park

Occupying three old burial grounds, including that of St Botolph's Aldersgate, this has been a public garden since 1880. It's best known for its Memorial to Heroic Self Sacrifice, the brainchild of George Frederic Watts (1817-1904), a Victorian painter, sculptor and philanthropist who wished to commemorate ordinary people who had died saving the lives of others. His memorial comprises a series of plaques on a wall beneath a loggia, recording heart-rending acts of selfless sacrifice: rescues from burning buildings, sinking ships and runaway horses. Reading them is an inspiring and humbling experience.

of peasants against punitive taxes, which fizzled out when the Mayor of London, William Walworth, stabbed rebel leader Wat Tyler to death.

Barbican Estate

This vast (40-acre/16ha) residential complex was built during the '60s and '70s in an area devastated by World War Two bombs. It's now Grade II listed and a prominent example of British Brutalist concrete architecture. It's home to the mighty Barbican Centre, Europe's largest arts and conference centre, constructed in 1982 as the City's gift to the nation at a cost of £161 million. At first glance, the Barbican is the original concrete jungle, but look closer and you'll discover that around one-third of the estate is given over to public and private gardens, ponds and a glorious conservatory.

To the east of the garden is one of the City's oldest churches, **St Bartholomew the Great ❺** and its tiny churchyard garden. With a rich history, interesting architecture, artworks and interior features, it's worth the price of admission (around £5). A priory church was first established here in 1123 as part of a monastery

of Augustinian canons and the site has been in continuous use as a place of worship ever since. The church entrance is opposite West Smithfield through a lovely medieval gate surmounted by a half-timbered Tudor building.

41-42 Cloth Fair

On leaving the church turn right into **Cloth Fair ❻**, the City's oldest street, where in medieval times merchants gathered to buy and sell material during the Bartholomew Fair. Take a look at numbers 41 & 42, the oldest residential dwellings in London; no 43 next door is the former home of poet John Betjeman, after whom the restaurant on the ground floor is named after. Continue along Cloth Fair into Middle Street, turning left at the end and right along Long Lane. Cross over at the junction with Aldersgate Street, turn right into Beech Street and right again into Lauderdale Place and the **Barbican Estate ❼** (see box). The estate's relentless concrete structures are softened by oases of lawn, flowerbeds and water, linked by a network of walkways and terraces, with waterside seating and panoramic views.

Barbican, Lakeside Terrace

City of London Parks & Gardens

From Lauderdale Place take the stairs on the left and follow the signs to the **Barbican Centre** 8 along the walkway past the private (residents') gardens on the right. At the end of the walkway go down the stairs to the **Lakeside Terrace** 9, a peaceful spot with a number of cafés and restaurants. Enter the Barbican Centre by the door just before the restaurant and take the stairs (or lift) to the 2nd floor (Library), turn right past the Osteria restaurant and right again over the Gilbert Bridge, which offers lovely views of the terrace.

Over the bridge take the stairs on the right down to St Giles Terrace and **St Giles Cripplegate** 10, a beautiful Grade I listed church; dating from 1394, it's one of few medieval churches left in the City. Behind the church is a peaceful terrace with benches, a

---

Barber-Surgeons

In medieval times, barber-surgeons were the medics of the battlefield. The link between barbers and surgeons wasn't broken until the 18th century, and the red and white pole outside a barber's shop recalls their more gory glory days – red for blood and white for bandages.

---

pond and a section of the Roman London Wall. Exit the Barbican Centre into Fore Street (just past Wood Street Bar & Restaurant) and turn left to discover **Salters' Hall and Garden** 11 – the entrance is around 100m along on the right. This secluded garden – sunk below road level with the old Roman City Wall as its southern boundary – is formally laid out with

areas of lawn, hedging, pergolas and fountains.

St Alphage Garden

Retrace your steps along Fore Street, turn left into Wood Street and take the first left to **St Alphage Garden** 12 (the street has the same name). A public garden since the 1870s, it contains the ruins of the church's 14th-century tower, flowerbeds, trees and seating. It's bounded on the north side by a high section of the old Roman wall, which forms the boundary with the adjacent Salters' Garden, visible through a gate.

Return to Wood Street and cross over to Monkwell Square. Walk around the square, past the Barber-Surgeons' Hall, and go up the stairs at the end – to the right, beside the road, a winding path leads to the entrance of the **Barber-Surgeons' Hall Gardens** 13. There has been a garden here since at least the 1550s, but this one was only created in 1987. It contains the Worshipful Company of Barbers' physic garden, with around 45 different species of plants used to treat wounds, bruises and burns, some of which still have an application in modern medicine. The garden also contains commemorative trees, including a yellow magnolia

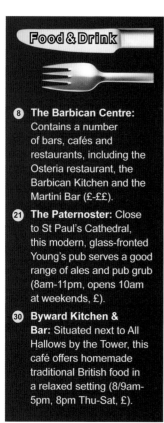

Food & Drink

8 **The Barbican Centre:** Contains a number of bars, cafés and restaurants, including the Osteria restaurant, the Barbican Kitchen and the Martini Bar (£-££).

21 **The Paternoster:** Close to St Paul's Cathedral, this modern, glass-fronted Young's pub serves a good range of ales and pub grub (8am-11pm, opens 10am at weekends, £).

30 **Byward Kitchen & Bar:** Situated next to All Hallows by the Tower, this café offers homemade traditional British food in a relaxed setting (8/9am-5pm, 8pm Thu-Sat, £).

planted for the Queen's Golden Jubilee in 2002, a large pond at the end and sections of the Roman London Wall, including the remains of a medieval tower.

Returning to London Wall, turn left and take the first right down Wood Street. Just past the tower of St Alban's church – the church was destroyed in the Blitz and its surviving tower is now a private dwelling – take the first left into Love Lane. Here, you'll find the lovely **St Mary Aldermanbury Garden** **14** on the left, opposite the medieval **Guildhall** **15**, home to the City of London Corporation. Like many City churches, St Mary Aldermanbury was destroyed in the Great Fire of 1666, rebuilt (by Wren) and finally finished off during the Blitz. The ruins are now a striking garden with areas of lawn, flowers and shrubs, a variety of trees and an ornamental box-hedged knot garden. The garden contains a bust of Shakespeare that commemorates two of his acting troupe – John Heminges and Henry Condell – both buried at St Mary's. After the Bard's death in 1616, they collected his works and published them at their own expense; without them we might not know who Shakespeare was!

Retrace your steps back to Wood Street and enter St Alban's Court opposite and follow it round into Oat Lane to **St Mary Staining Churchyard** **16**. The church was lost in the Great Fire in 1666

St Mary Aldermanbury Garden

and the land lay derelict until 1965 when the City of London Corporation laid out a garden, consisting of a raised area of lawn with a large plane tree, flowerbeds and shrubs; tombstones are ranged along the back, and the garden is overlooked by the Pewterers' Hall. Back on Oat Lane, follow the road left into Staining Lane and turn right at the end into Gresham Street. On the right is the **St John Zachary Garden** ⑰ , aka the Goldsmiths' Garden (the gold leopard's heads on the pillars are the hallmark of the Goldsmiths Company Assay Office). It occupies the site of the medieval church of St John Zachary, which was damaged in the Great Fire. First laid out as a sunken garden in 1941, the garden contains lawns, trees and a fountain, plus an unusual sculpture, **The Three Printers** ⑱ (ca. 1957 by Wilfred Dudeney), which represents the newspaper industry, depicting a newsboy, a typesetter and an editor.

Cross Noble Street to visit **St Anne & St Agnes Church** ⑲ and its lovely garden, created in the '70s with a lawn and a variety of trees including Indian bean, catalpa, false acacia, rowan and cherry. The original church was destroyed in the Great Fire and a new church, designed by Wren, was largely completed in 1681. It was damaged in World War Two but was restored in keeping with Wren's design. Exiting St Anne & St Agnes, turn right and then left down St Martin's Le Grand and cross over Newgate Street at the end (towards St Paul's tube

St Paul's Cathedral

An Anglican cathedral and the seat of the Bishop of London, St Paul's sits atop the City's highest hill (Ludgate) and at 365ft (111m) it was, until 1962, the tallest structure in London – its dome still dominates the skyline. Designed by Sir Christopher Wren, the English Baroque masterpiece is the fifth church to stand here – the first dated from 604AD – and was built between 1675 and 1710 after its predecessor was destroyed in the Great Fire. The Cathedral (high entrance fee) has a bookshop, café and restaurant.

station). Around 50m further on along Panyer Alley is **St Paul's Churchyard Garden** ⑳ . If you're ready for lunch or a drink, **The Paternoster** 21 pub in nearby Paternoster Square is worth a visit.

Sir Christopher Wren's iconic cathedral is encircled by lovely

St Paul's Churchyard Garden

Thomas Becket statue

gardens (around 2.5 acres/1ha), laid out in 1879 on the old burial grounds of **St Paul's Cathedral** 22 (see box) and its neighbouring churches. Designed by Edward Milner, the garden contains winding footpaths, fountains, sculpture and seating, and features lawns and mature trees and shrubs, as well as a lovely rose garden. Among the many specimen trees are ginkgo, maple, lime, ash, mulberry and eucalyptus, as well as some of the oldest plane trees in London and the City's only giant fir. The gardens also contain several monuments, including a reproduction of Francis Bird's statue of Queen Anne – the reigning monarch when the cathedral was completed in 1712 – and a granite memorial to 'the people of London 1939-1945' who were less fortunate than the cathedral in avoiding destruction during the Blitz. There's also a fine resin statue by Edward Bainbridge Copnall (1970) of Thomas Becket, Archbishop of Canterbury 1162-1170, who was murdered in Canterbury Cathedral.

Exit the churchyard garden to the southeast into the award-winning **Festival Gardens** 23 . Designed by Sir Albert Richardson, they were the Corporation of London's contribution to the Festival of Britain in 1951. The gardens consist of a sunken lawn with a

Young Lovers

wall fountain (with water flowing from lions' mouths), donated by the Worshipful Company of Gardeners, a raised paved terrace with stone parapets and seating, and a number of trees, including a lime 'hedge' and a fine catalpa tree. Look out for the statue, The Young Lovers, by Georg Ehrlich (1951), in front of the fountain. To the west of the Gardens is the Queen's Diamond Jubilee Garden, formerly a coach park, which was

---

St Mary Aldermary

St Mary Aldermary (Grade I listed, open 11am-3pm) is an ashlar-faced 17th-century Anglican church with a gorgeous interior, rebuilt by Wren in Gothic style after the Great Fire. According to art expert Nikolaus Pevsner, St Mary Aldermary is 'the chief surviving monument of the 17th-century Gothic revival in the City and (along with the Collegiate Church of St Mary, Warwick) is the most important late 17th-century Gothic church in England.'

City of London Parks & Gardens

transformed in 2012 into a swathe of green, boasting a large lawn, some 3,000 herbaceous plants, around 200m of clipped box hedging, flowering street trees and multi-stemmed garden trees. At the east end of the garden is a fine Nigel Boonham bust of John Donne (1572-1631), one of England's foremost poets and priests (former Dean of St Paul's), unveiled in 2012.

Cleary Garden

From Festival Gardens cross over New Change to **25 Cannon Street Gardens** ㉔ , an award-winning contemporary half-acre garden created in 2000. It's a

secluded space, with an oval, slightly convex lawn surrounded by trees, shrubs and herbaceous planting.

Cross Cannon Street outside number 25 to take Friday Street and turn left on Queen Victoria Street. Opposite is **Cleary Garden** ㉕ , a peaceful hillside garden set back from the road. Its three tiers reveal an intriguing history, from Blitz bomb damage on the upper section, through medieval London by the stairway, and a section that covers the site of a Roman bathhouse at the lower level. The garden was built in the rubble of a bombed-out house in the '40s, and named after Fred Cleary, who was instrumental in encouraging the creation of new gardens throughout the City. The garden

has shaded wooden arbours, a lovely pergola, and a sunny terrace with a miniature vineyard – a throwback to medieval times when this area was a hub of the wine trade. It provides a variety of wildlife habitats: sparrows and blue tits nest in the buddleia, and greenfinches, robins, blackbirds and dunnocks are frequent visitors.

Leaving Cleary Garden continue east along Queen Victoria Street (passing Mansion House tube station) until you're back on Cannon Street. Take a brief detour up Bow Lane to visit **St Mary Aldermary** ㉖ (see box), then continue east along Cannon Street and turn right down Queen Street and left at the end into Upper Thames Street. A short distance up on your left is our next stop, **Whittington Garden** ㉗ , named after Richard 'Dick' Whittington, one of the most famous Lord Mayors of London. The garden sits alongside the church of St Michael Paternoster Royal, which Whittington had rebuilt at his own expense in 1409; he was buried there in 1423 and the church has a lovely stained-glass window commemorating him. The garden was laid out in 1960 with a largely paved area in the west, and grass, flowerbeds and trees in the east. A small fountain was erected in the west section in the late '60s.

Continue down Upper Thames Street under **Cannon Street Station** 28 and London Bridge to Lower Thames Street – you pass St Magnus the Martyr and the Old Billingsgate (fish) market hall on your right. As the street curves to the left – just past Billingsgate Roman House and Baths, tucked away behind a modern façade – turn up St Dunstan's Hill on your left. This leads to **St Dunstan-in-the-East Garden** 29 (see box),

Abbey of Barking in 675AD. It's well worth a look and has a marvellous café next door, the Byward Kitchen & Bar.

St Dunstan-in-the-East Garden

Although a church has stood here since at least the 12th century, St Dunstan was virtually destroyed in the Blitz. In 1967, the Grade I listed ruins – which include a tower by Wren – and former churchyard were incorporated into a glorious garden. The walls and majestic windows are draped with Virginia creeper and ornamental vine, while exotic plants such as pineapple-scented Moroccan broom and New Zealand flax thrive in the sheltered conditions. In the lower garden is a Japanese snowball that displays breath-taking blossom in late spring.

St Dunstan-in-the-East Garden

one of the City's most delightfully melancholic gardens.

Leaving St Dunstan, turn down Cross Lane back to Lower Thames Street and east into Byward Street. On your right is the magnificent **All Hallows by the Tower** 30 , the oldest church in the City, founded by the

Continue past the church until you come to our next stop, **Trinity Square Gardens** 31 , which were laid out in 1795 as the setting for Trinity House (1796), the HQ of the General Lighthouse Authority. The gardens contain the poignant **Tower Hill Memorial** 32 to

seamen who lost their lives in the world wars 'who have no grave but the sea'; it incorporates the WWI Mercantile Marine Memorial by Sir Edwin Lutyens and the WWII Merchant Seamen's

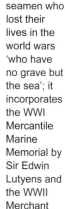

City of London Parks & Gardens

Seething Lane Gardens

Memorial by Sir Edward Maufe, laid out in the form of a sunken garden. Also within the gardens, less heroic and rather gruesome, is the **Execution Memorial** ㉝ (see box).

Leaving Trinity Square Gardens, take Muscovy Street on the western side and turn right into Seething Lane and **Seething Lane Gardens** ㉞. This was the site of the Navy Office where Samuel Pepys once worked – look for the bronze bust of the eminent diarist by Karin Jonzen – and where Pepys reportedly buried his wine and Parmesan cheese to protect them from the Great Fire! The simple rectangular garden is bounded by railings and laid out symmetrically with a central path, well shaded by trees, with rose beds either side of the gates. Continue a little way along Seething Lane to reach our final stop, **St Olave's Garden** ㉟, on the left-hand side. Grade I listed, St Olave's is a medieval church dedicated to the patron saint of Norway (St Olaf), but is best known as the resting place of Pepys, who was buried in the nave in 1703 next to his wife Elisabeth. The garden is also the final resting place of 16th-century botanist, William Turner, known as

> ### Execution Memorial
>
> This modest brick-pavel memorial in Trinity Square marks the location of the scaffold on Tower Hill, where more than 125 people were put to death between the 14th and 18th centuries. Around the edge of the memorial are plaques listing the names of the dead, including some of Henry VIII's victims such as Sir Thomas More and Thomas Cromwell. The names of Henry's wives aren't included as they were executed privately inside the Tower of London, rather than endure the public spectacle of an execution on Tower Hill.

'the father of English botany', and was recently replanted with plants associated with him.

Leaving the garden via Seething Lane, turn left and left again into Hart Street and right into Mark Lane. The next right takes you into London Street and to Fenchurch Street Station, which marks the end of this walk. Or if you prefer, you can retrace your steps to Trinity Square Gardens and Tower Hill tube.

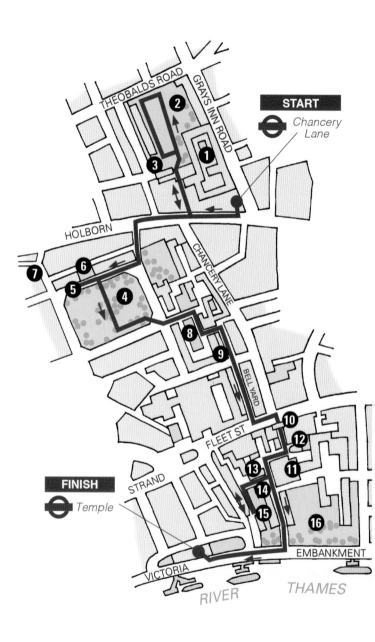

START
Chancery Lane

THEOBALDS ROAD

GRAYS INN ROAD

HOLBORN

CHANCERY LANE

BELL YARD

FLEET ST

STRAND

FINISH
Temple

VICTORIA

EMBANKMENT

RIVER THAMES

● Places of Interest ● Food & Drink

WALK 9

Inns of Court Gardens

Distance: 2mi (3.2km)

Terrain: easy, flat terrain

Duration: 1-2 hours

Open: See box below

Start: Chancery Lane tube

End: Temple tube

Postcode: WC1V 6DR

The four Inns of Court – Gray's Inn, Lincoln's Inn, Inner Temple and Middle Temple – are the professional associations for barristers in England and Wales. They are important organisations with supervisory and disciplinary functions over their members, and anyone wishing to train for the Bar must join one of them. Each Inn is a self-contained precinct where barristers train and practise, providing its members with libraries, dining facilities, accommodation, chambers, a meeting hall, church or chapel – and glorious gardens in which to contemplate the law.

The Inns – the term comes from their origins as hostelries for law students – have a long and fascinating history. Lawyers took over the Inner and Middle Temples in the mid-14th century from the Knights Templar who had occupied the site since the 12th century, while Lincoln's Inn and Gray's Inn date from around the same time, and were associated with Henry de Lacy, Earl of Lincoln, and Reginald le Gray, Chief Justice of Chester, respectively.

The Inns resemble Oxbridge colleges in their layout, which can extend to several acres. And while most buildings are closed to the public, the gardens, courtyards, squares and walks are open to everyone, and provide essential 'green lungs' for lawyers, office workers and tourists. With their lofty image and ancient traditions, the Inns are very rewarding to explore, as you walk in the footsteps of legal and literary giants of the past, from Pepys and Dickens to Shakespeare and Lamb.

Due to the limited opening hours (see box right) of the Inns of Court gardens, you should start this walk no later than 11.30am in order to have sufficient time to explore all four gardens. Note that Middle Temple

Inns of Court Gardens

Gardens are open only in May to July and September.

of open parkland, dotted with specimen trees and plants. Allées of pleached trees (where the branches are interlaced to form a hedge or provide a walkway) and a formal garden were hallmarks of the original plantings. Today, the main feature is a broad gravel path between an avenue of young red oak trees (planted in 1990) and majestic London planes. There are also informally

Start Walking…

Leave Chancery Lane tube station via exit 1 to Gray's Inn Road, taking a moment to admire Staple Inn on the opposite side of High Holborn. Built in 1545, it was one of the few buildings to survive the Great Fire of 1666 and is now home to Caffè Vergnano 1882 – the perfect place to get your morning caffeine kick. Turn right and head west along High Holborn, passing the main entrance to **Gray's Inn** ❶ and the historic Cittie of York pub. A short distance past the pub, turn right into Fulwood Place and walk to the top to the entrance to **Gray's Inn Gardens** ❷. At 5.8 acres (2.3ha), this is one of the largest privately owned gardens in London and was laid out by Sir Francis Bacon (see box) in 1606. The elegant wrought-iron gates feature pillars with griffins standing guard; dating from 1723, they feature the initials of the Treasurer at that time, William Gylby.

Gray's Inn Gardens, also known as the Walks, give the impression

Gray's Inn Gardens

Sir Francis Bacon

Sir Francis Bacon (1561-1626) had a long involvement with Gray's Inn. He was admitted to the Inn in 1576 and called to the Bar in 1582; he was later elected Treasurer of the Inn in 1608 and held the position until 1617, when he was appointed Lord Privy Seal. A statue (1912) of Sir Francis by F. W. Pomeroy stands in the South Square within the precincts. Sadly, Bacon's career ended in disgrace in 1621, when he was convicted of corruption, fined £40,000, and imprisoned in the Tower of London.

In 1701, the Walks were the scene of a duel between Captain Greenwood and Mr Ottway. The unfortunate encounter resulted in the death of Mr Ottway and the trial of Captain Greenwood and his subsequent conviction for manslaughter.

arranged hawthorn, copper beech and catalpa (Indian bean trees, planted by Bacon). The north bank of the Walks is particularly delightful in spring when it glows with the yellow of thousands of daffodils, followed by summery ox-eye daisies. Roses climb the railings, while herbaceous and herb borders provide colour and fragrance. On the lawn south of the Atkin Building (left of the entrance) is **The Bronze Angel** ❸, a statue by Geoffrey Wickham installed in 2012.

The Walks are a popular lunchtime retreat, and on sunny days the lawns are packed, as are the numerous memorial benches. From the gardens, retrace your steps to High Holborn, cross to the south side, turn right and walk westwards; after 200m turn left into Great Turnstile (there was indeed a turnstile here in the 1600s) and Newman's Row, passing Lincoln's Inn on your left.

Lincoln's Inn Fields ❹ (see box) is London's largest garden square (7.25 acres/2.9ha) with a history dating back to the 12th century. On the north side is **Sir John Soane's Museum** ❻, one of London's most intriguing museums, showcasing the famous architect's (1753-1837) eclectic collection displayed in his former home (www.soane.org). A bit further along at no 71 is the **Fleet River Bakery** ❼, which serves superior coffee, cakes and savoury dishes.

Leave the square via the southeast corner onto Serle Street, and almost directly opposite is the main entrance to **Lincoln's Inn** ❽. The Inn was founded around 1422, on land bequeathed to the legal fraternity by the Earl of Lincoln, and its Old Hall dates back to the late 15th

Lincoln's Inn Fields

Designed as a residential garden square by Inigo Jones in 1618, this has been the site of jousting, notorious duels and the occasional public execution (Lord William Russell was beheaded – rather messily – here in 1688). The Fields have been a municipal public garden since 1895 (open 7.30am to dusk) and comprise shrubberies, flowerbeds, tennis courts and an octagonal pavilion/bandstand. Trees include catalpa, ginkgo, holly, mountain ash and laburnum, and there are some interesting memorials. To the right of the central north entrance is a lovely bronze by Richard R. Goulden: **Memorial to Margaret MacDonald** ❺ depicts the social reformer and wife of Ramsay MacDonald, who lived at 3 Lincoln's Inn Fields.

Lincoln's Inn Fields

century. Formal gardens were created in the 16th century but these have been much altered over the centuries. Today, Lincoln's Inn Gardens consist of six separate gardens: the North Lawn (open noon-2.30pm), Benchers' Lawn, New Square (some 300 years old!), Gatehouse Court, Kitchen Garden and Stone Buildings. The atmosphere is tranquil for such a busy corner of London, and ancient trees and lush lawns offer a haven for wildlife. Visitors are welcome to walk around the precincts of the Inn, which are open 7am to 7pm on weekdays (the Inn's buildings are open only for organised tours, except for the chapel, which opens Mon-Fri, 9am-5pm).

Lincoln's Inn

Exit the gardens from the eastern side of New Square through the Kitchen Garden, where you turn right to Bishop's Court and right again into Star Yard. The yard boasts a Grade II listed green urinal, in the style of a Parisian *pissoir* – a common sight in 19th-century London – and is home to Ede & Ravenscroft, London's oldest tailor, established in 1689 and specialising in legal wigs and gowns. Continue along Star Yard, crossing over Carey Street into Bell Yard, past the Law Society building on the left, to Fleet Street. On the corner is the magnificent **Old Bank of England** 9 pub – worth a visit just to gawp at the décor.

Cross over Fleet Street and go left to no 17 – **Prince Henry's Room** 10 – dating from before the Great Fire and reportedly used by Henry (1594-1612), son of James I. Pass through the narrow doorway beneath the 'room' into Inner Temple Lane and the precincts of the **Inner Temple** 11. On the left is the atmospheric 12th-century **Temple Church** 12 (entrance fee £5, £3 concessions), the first Gothic church built in London (1160-1185). This is where, in the 13th century, novices were initiated into the order of the Knights Templar, the Catholic military order formed in 1118 to protect pilgrims in the Holy Land.

When the Knights Templar order was dissolved in 1312, the site passed to the Knights Hospitaller and then, in 1608, to the barristers (courtesy of James I). Overlooking the River Thames, the gardens with their sweeping lawns, lavish floral

Old Bank of England

displays and elegant courtyards, are thought to date back to the 12th century when the Knights Templar first arrived, although they have been reworked and enlarged over the last 900 years. Both the Inner and Middle Temple gardens are peaceful retreats, attracting plenty of wildlife, from bees and butterflies in the borders, to nesting birds such as robins, thrushes, coal tits and blue tits.

> ### Middle Temple Hall
>
> This is one of the finest surviving Elizabethan halls in Britain with a double hammer beam roof carved from the oaks of Windsor Forest and a 29ft (8.8m) bench table, believed to have been a gift from Elizabeth I. The Hall was the venue for the first performance of Shakespeare's *Twelfth Night* in 1601 – nowadays it's possible for the hoi polloi to enjoy lunch here (bookings 020-7427 4820).

Middle Temple Hall & Gardens

With Temple Church on your left, go straight ahead under the colonnade, through the archway and down some steps to pretty Elm Court and continue into **Fountain Court** ⓭ past **Middle Temple Hall** ⓮ (see box) on your left. The court reputedly has the oldest permanent fountain in London (dating from 1681), and is where Ruth Pinch met John Westlock in Dickens' *Martin Chuzzlewit*. At the end of the court turn left down some stairs, where the entrance to **Middle Temple Gardens** ⓯ is on your left. The gardens look much as they did in the 1870s when they were enlarged following the creation of the Victoria Embankment. In the southern half of the lawn is a circular flowerbed with a sundial from 1719 at its centre, and a statue of a boy holding a book, erected in 1930 in memory of the children's author Charles Lamb (1775-1834), who was born in the Inner Temple. The northern part of the garden (below Middle Temple Hall) has terraced bedding displays – look for a small bed containing the roses of York and Lancaster.

Retrace your steps back to Fountain Court and turn right past Middle Temple Hall into Middle Temple Lane and left under the elaborate stone archway opposite. The entrance to **Inner Temple Garden** ⓰ (3 acres/1.2ha) is through some impressively decorated gates (1730) on the right, embellished with a griffin and Pegasus from the coats of arms of Gray's Inn and the Inner

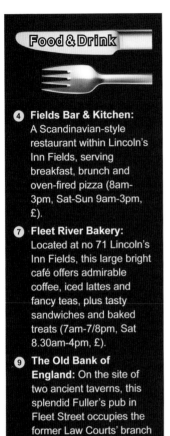

4 Fields Bar & Kitchen: A Scandinavian-style restaurant within Lincoln's Inn Fields, serving breakfast, brunch and oven-fired pizza (8am-3pm, Sat-Sun 9am-3pm, £).

7 Fleet River Bakery: Located at no 71 Lincoln's Inn Fields, this large bright café offers admirable coffee, iced lattes and fancy teas, plus tasty sandwiches and baked treats (7am-7/8pm, Sat 8.30am-4pm, £).

9 The Old Bank of England: On the site of two ancient taverns, this splendid Fuller's pub in Fleet Street occupies the former Law Courts' branch of the Bank of England. Serves a good range of beers and traditional pub grub (Mon-Fri, 11am-11pm, Sat noon-9pm, £).

black mulberry, fruiting walnut and medlar.

Seasonal planting ensures that the magnificent borders are a riot of colour from spring to autumn – snowdrops, daffodils, bluebells, tulips, roses, poppies, geraniums and dahlias, to name just a few – plus a peony garden, woodland garden and an area of Mediterranean planting. The result is a thoroughly English garden and a haven of tranquility – the Royal Horticultural Society held its Great Spring Show here from 1888 to 1913, before moving to Chelsea where it became the Chelsea Flower Show.

When you've have had your fill of the gardens, leave via the main gate, turn left into Middle Temple Lane towards the Embankment and right for Temple tube station, passing Victoria Embankment Gardens on the way (see **Walk 10**).

Inner Temple Garden

Temple respectively. The garden has extensive lawns and scattered trees, including catalpa, ailanthus, flowering cherry, sorbus, cedar, magnolia and ginkgo, while fruit trees recall the medieval orchards once planted here, including a

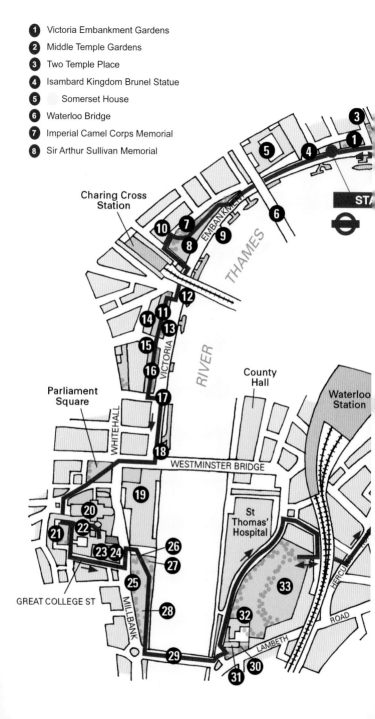

1 Victoria Embankment Gardens
2 Middle Temple Gardens
3 Two Temple Place
4 Isambard Kingdom Brunel Statue
5 Somerset House
6 Waterloo Bridge
7 Imperial Camel Corps Memorial
8 Sir Arthur Sullivan Memorial

Charing Cross Station

STA

THAMES

RIVER

EMBANKMENT

Parliament Square

County Hall

Waterloo Station

WHITEHALL

WESTMINSTER BRIDGE

St Thomas' Hospital

VICTORIA

GREAT COLLEGE ST

MILLBANK

LAMBETH

ROAD

HERCU

2

RT

Temple

FINISH

Lambeth North

● Places of Interest   ○ Food & Drink

Thameside Gardens

WALK 10

Distance: 3¼mi (5¼km)

Terrain: easy

Duration: 2 hours

Open: Most daily, dawn to dusk

Start: Temple tube

End: Lambeth North tube

Postcode: WC2R 2PH

THAMESIDE GARDENS

This walk takes you north to south along the Thames between Blackfriars and Lambeth Bridges, through a network of riverside gardens, many created as a by-product of the construction of London's sewerage system in the mid-19th century – a remarkable feat of Victorian civil engineering by Sir Joseph Bazalgette. During the excavation work along the Thames, some 32 acres of reclaimed land were transformed into the new Embankment and the series of gardens we see today. These gardens – from Victoria Embankment Gardens to Victoria Tower Gardens – provide a welcome retreat from the city's bustling streets.

All have gravel or tarmac paths lined with seats, many donated as memorials. They are delightful and varied spaces, green with lawns and mature trees, scattered with flowerbeds and dotted with striking statues, monuments and memorials, street furniture, cafés and play areas for children. They provide a vital refuge for the city's wildlife, too.

Along the way we also take in the gardens of Westminster Abbey, the Garden Museum and Archbishop's Park, while passing some of London's most famous buildings, including Somerset House, the Palace of Westminster and Westminster Abbey, not forgetting the many iconic bridges.

Victoria Embankment Gardens

Start Walking…

Exiting from Temple tube station turn left to visit the first of four sections of the **Victoria Embankment Gardens** ❶ (7.30am to dusk daily). The gardens opened in 1874 and extend to 11 acres (4.5ha) along the north side of the Thames between Blackfriars and Westminster Bridges. They were designed by Alexander McKenzie and created in four sections: the Temple Garden to the northeast, the Main Gardens in the middle between Hungerford and Waterloo Bridges, and two sections (Whitehall Gardens and the Ministry of Defence) to the south.

The Temple Garden, adjacent to the **Middle Temple Gardens** ❷ (see **Walk 9**), is a small, quiet corner shaded by plane trees and shrubs. It contains a charming memorial to Lady Henry Somerset – wife of Lord Somerset – philanthropist, temperance leader and campaigner for women's rights. Just behind the garden is **Two Temple Place** ❸, a Gothic Revival extravaganza built in 1895 for William Waldorf Astor (open during periodic exhibitions or by appointment).

Leaving the garden, go right past Temple tube station to the entrance to Temple Place, where there's a fine statue (hidden by a canopy of trees) by Carlo Marochetti of Victorian engineer **Isambard Kingdom Brunel** ❹ – considered by many to be England's finest ever engineer – standing on a small plot of land that's now part of

> ### Somerset House
>
> Former home of the Royal Academy of Arts, Somerset House is now a centre for the visual arts and hosts open-air concerts, film screenings and art exhibitions. It also houses the splendid Courtauld Gallery, which has a gem of an art collection, ranging from early Renaissance to 20th-century modernist works. During the summer months, 55 fountains dance in the magnificent courtyard, while in winter it becomes one of London's favourite ice rinks. There are a number of excellent cafés (try Fernandez & Wells), restaurants and bars.

Victoria Embankment Gardens. Crossing over Temple Place you pass **Somerset House** 5 (see box), a spectacular 18th-century Neoclassical building designed by William Chambers (1723-1796). Opposite the house is the RNLI Thames Lifeboat Station, originally built to rescue would-be suicides jumping off Waterloo Bridge.

Continuing under **Waterloo Bridge** ❻ you come to the main section of the Victoria Embankment Gardens (once called the Adelphi Gardens), noted for their outstanding bedding displays throughout the year and majestic trees. There's a café

Imperial Camel Corps Memorial

Whitehall Gardens

and a bandstand here, where concerts are held in summer and deckchairs are for hire. Statues include a small but elegant memorial to the **Imperial Camel Corps** ❼ by Major Cecil Brown, figures of Robert Burns (Scots poet) and Robert Raikes (the founder of Sunday schools), and a superb statue by William Goscombe John of **Sir Arthur Sullivan** ❽, the composer who worked with Sir William Gilbert (who has his own memorial near Embankment Pier). Another popular statue is a bronze Figure on a Drinking Fountain of a young girl holding a bowl in front of her, sculpted by George Edward Wade and a tribute to Lady Henry Somerset (mentioned above).

Around the middle point of the park, on Victoria Embankment, is **Cleopatra's Needle** ❾, an obelisk dating from around 1450BC. A gift from the ruler of

Egypt, it was erected here in 1877. It's complimented by some eye-catching, Egyptian-themed benches made of cast iron and dating from the mid-1870s. The benches feature either sphinxes or camels and were designed by George John Vulliamy, architect of the Board of Works, who was also responsible for the 'dolphin' lamp-posts along the river and the Needle's pedestal and sphinxes.

At the end of the Embankment Gardens is the **York Watergate** ❿ (see box), curiously marooned 150m from the river, while at the rear of the gardens are two striking Art Deco office blocks: the Adelphi, built in the late '30s, with Shell-Mex House (1931) to the right of it, noted for its massive squat clock tower. On the right of Shell-Mex House is the iconic Savoy Hotel, built in 1889.

York Watergate

An intriguing reminder of a time when a string of mansions lined the Strand and backed onto the Thames, the York Watergate is all that remains of York House (as it later became), built as a London base for the Bishops of Norwich, probably in the 1230s. The Watergate was built around 1625 to provide a place for the Duke of Buckingham to alight from his boat, but now sits 150m back from the river – a stark indication of just how much land was claimed by the construction of the Thames Embankment.

Battle of Britain Memorial

At the end of this section of the garden you pass under the Hungerford and Golden Jubilee foot bridges (flanking a railway bridge), adjacent to Embankment tube station. Beyond the bridges is **Whitehall Gardens** ⓫ , laid out in 1875 by Vulliamy. Opposite, on the Embankment, is a memorial by George Simmons to **Sir Joseph Bazalgette** ⓬ (1819-1891), the eminent Victorian engineer; above the bronze bust are the words: *Flumini vincula posuit* (He chained the river). The gardens contain a wonderful array of shrubbery, bedding displays, mature London plane trees, lime trees and trees of heaven. There are many statues and monuments here, including a striking **Memorial to Samuel Plimsoll** ⓭ – who devised the Plimsoll line on a ship's hull which shows its maximum safe draft – on the Thames side of the gardens (opposite boat-turned-bar-restaurant the *Tattershall Castle*). At the rear of the gardens is the splendid Grade I listed **Royal Horseguards Hotel** ⓮ ,

constructed in 1884 and modelled on a French chateau.

Leaving Whitehall Gardens, cross Horse Guards Avenue to the final section of Victoria Embankment Gardens, dominated by the Ministry of Defence building. Preserved in the northwest corner of the gardens are the remains of the old Whitehall Steps to the Thames, also known as the **'Queen Mary Steps'** ⓯ – built for Mary II in 1691 by Sir Christopher Wren – together with the early 16th-century Thames Embankment wall. Discovered in 1939, these are the only existing remains of Whitehall Palace, the residence of Tudor monarchs.

Monuments in this section include one to General Charles George Gordon 'of Khartoum' (1833-1885); the **Fleet Air Arm Memorial** ⓰ (aka Daedalus) by James Butler; and the Royal Air Force Memorial topped with a golden eagle on the Embankment (1923) opposite the FAA memorial. However, the most spectacular and dramatic monument on the

Embankment – at the end of the gardens – is the striking **Battle of Britain Memorial**  ⑰. Installed in 2005 on the 65th anniversary of the battle, its centrepiece is 'Scramble', depicting airmen running towards their planes to

College Garden

intercept enemy aircraft. Conceived by Bill Bond and sculpted by Paul Day, the monument is engraved with all 2,936 names of the British and allied airmen who fought in the

College Garden

This garden, belonging to Westminster Abbey since the 11th century, is said to be the oldest in England under continuous cultivation. The oldest surviving features visible today are the 14th-century stone precinct walls at the far end and along the left-hand side as you stand at the entrance gate, and the four weathered statues of the apostles, carved in 1686 by Grinling Gibbons and formerly in the Palace of Whitehall. The garden is dominated by five tall plane trees, planted in 1850, while other specimen trees include quince, step-over apple trees (at the entrance) and a white mulberry near the fountain.

battle. From here there's a superb view of the London Eye and City Hall on the opposite bank.

From the Battle of Britain Monument walk south past Westminster Pier where, on a pedestal to the right of the steps just before Westminster Bridge, is an impressive bronze statue by Thomas Thorneycroft of **Queen Boadicea** ⑱ and her daughters driving a war chariot. Boadicea (Boudicca) was queen of the Celtic Iceni tribe who led an uprising against the Romans in around AD60. Cross the road and turn right, passing the **Palace of Westminster** ⑲ (Houses of Parliament) to Parliament Square, where there are some interesting statues, including those of Winston Churchill, Mahatma Gandhi and Viscount Palmerston. Cross over the square and go past St Margaret's Church and **Westminster Abbey** ⑳ into Broad Sanctuary and bear left into The Sanctuary, where – to the right of the Abbey – is an arch leading into **Dean's Yard** ㉑, a handsome square built on the site of the former monastery's farmyard. The broad lawns provide a centrepiece for the picturesque 'collegiate' architecture of Dean's Yard, partly designed by George Gilbert Scott. It has a number of mature trees, including London planes, a red horse chestnut and a tulip tree.

Our next gardens are literally hidden gems, secreted as they are within the precincts of Westminster

Abbey. They are restful retreats, where it's still possible to imagine the great church as the haunt of monks and pilgrims (rather than busloads of tourists), and are a delightful place to escape the crowded confines of the abbey – plus, you don't have to pay an archbishop's ransom to enjoy them, as entry is free!

Turn left as you enter Dean's Yard and in the northeast corner is the entrance to the **Cellarium Café** 22 and the gardens. There are four gardens within the Abbey precinct: the three original gardens (the Great Cloister Garden or Garth, the Little Cloister and College Garden) and St Catherine's Garden, which lies in the area of the ruined monastery and was created more recently. The Cloisters are open 8am-6pm in summer, 9.30am-4pm in winter, while College Garden opens Tue-Thu 10am-6pm, 4pm in winter. Each of the Abbey's gardens had a separate function: the Garth with its square of turf, bounded by Cloisters, provided the monks with somewhere to rest their eyes and minds as they walked around it, while the Little Cloister Garden – a small but charming courtyard garden, with borders of scented plants and a fountain – was reserved for recuperation after illness. The largest and most important garden is the **College Garden** 23 (see box) – 'college' refers to the old meaning of the word, i.e. a community of clergy – which, 1,000 years ago, was the infirmary garden of the monastery.

When you've explored the Abbey gardens turn left from the

exit into Dean's Yard and leave via the archway in the southeast corner into Great College Street. Turn left and follow the street to the end, passing the Jewel Tower and College Green – with Henry Moore's bronze **Knife Edge Two Piece** 24 (1962) in the middle – to Abingdon Street/Millbank and **Victoria Tower Gardens** 25 opposite. The entrance is around 20m to your left. The gardens (open dawn to dusk) stand in the shadow of Victoria Tower at the south-western corner of the Palace of Westminster, and extend south to Lambeth Bridge, sandwiched between Millbank and the Thames. They consist of a broad swathe of grass bordered by mature trees – mostly London planes – perfect for relaxing, reading or rehearsing a parliamentary speech (or, more likely, sleeping off a heavy lunch!). The gardens were laid out in 1864-70 and extended around 1914.

Being so close to the heart of British politics, it's perhaps inevitable that the statues in the gardens have a political theme. Opposite the entrance is a fine statue of suffragette **Emmeline Pankhurst** 26 (1858-1928), who endured many spells of

Buxton Memorial Fountain

This grand neo-Gothic confection commemorates the abolition of slavery in the British Empire in 1834. Commissioned by Charles Buxton MP – who campaigned against slavery in parliament – and designed by Samuel Sanders Teulon in 1865 (by coincidence, the same year that the US passed the 13th Amendment outlawing slavery), it originally stood in Parliament Square but has been here since 1957.

imprisonment to win women the right to vote. Sculpted by A. G. Walker, it was erected just two years after her death in 1928, a month before all adult women could finally vote in elections. Follow the path to the right and on the left is a cast of Auguste Rodin's magnificent bronze, **The Burghers of Calais** 27, completed in 1889 and installed here in 1915. It commemorates a pivotal moment in 1347 during the Hundred Years' War when the French port of Calais was under siege by the English, and six civic notables gave themselves up in an act of self-sacrifice to save their fellow townspeople (they were spared by Edward III). There's also a glorious fountain, the **Buxton Memorial Fountain** 28 (see box), at the far end of the gardens.

Leave Victoria Tower Gardens by the exit just past the fountain and cross **Lambeth Bridge** 29. The five-span steel arch bridge opened in 1932 and is painted red to match the seats in the House of Lords (Westminster Bridge, further downstream, is painted green to match the seats in the Commons). Over the bridge turn left and cross Lambeth Palace Road at the traffic lights to the **Garden Museum** 30. The museum (open daily 10.30am-5pm, Sat until 4pm) occupies the building and churchyard of the deconsecrated church of St Mary-at-Lambeth, dating from the 14th century. It was established to rescue the church from demolition following the discovery of the graves of two 17th-century royal gardeners and plant hunters, John Tradescant (father and son). Anne Boleyn's mother Elizabeth also rests here, as does William Bligh, captain of the infamous *Bounty*. In the former churchyard is a lovely recreated 17th-century knot garden, in a formal geometric style with authentic period planting. The museum was the world's first museum dedicated to the history of gardening, and celebrates British gardens and gardening. There's a fee to visit the museum but no charge for the superb vegetarian **Garden Café** 31 next door.

Next to the café is Morton's Tower (1490), the gatehouse that guards the entrance to **Lambeth Palace** 32, the London residence of the Archbishops of Canterbury for some 800 years. The palace and its gardens aren't open to the public but guided tours can

Food & Drink

5 **Fernandez & Wells:** Located in Somerset House, this café-bar is a great place for coffee, lunch or tapas and an early evening drink (8/9am-10/11pm and 6pm on Sundays, £).

22 **Cellarium Café & Terrace:** Westminster Abbey's café is set in the monks' original larder; fully licensed, it serves imaginative salads and tasty mains. Free access is provided via Dean's Yard (Mon-Fri, 8am, Sat-Sun 9-10am, closing time varies 4-7.30pm, £).

31 **Garden Café:** This highly-rated café offers fresh seasonal vegetarian and vegan food with a focus on simple, quality ingredients, making the most of the museum's kitchen garden (8am-5pm, lunch noon-3pm, £).

called **Archbishop's Park** **33** (7.30am to dusk) – from Morton's Tower, walk along Lambeth Palace Road skirting Lambeth Palace Gardens (with St Thomas' Hospital on your left) and turn right into Royal Street and right again into Carlisle Lane. The park contains a number of wildlife-friendly zones, including a community orchard, but the emphasis is very much on play, with facilities including an all-weather games area, tennis and netball courts, and a children's play area.

This marks the end of our walk. To get to Lambeth North tube station, turn left on Carlisle Lane and right into Virgil Street (under the railway tracks) and left on Hercules Road. At the end of the road turn left onto Kennington Road and you soon see the tube station on your right.

be booked through its website. A section of the palace grounds, formerly known as Lambeth Palace Field, was put aside as a children's playground after the death of Archbishop Tait in 1882, and opened as a public park in 1901. To get to the park – now

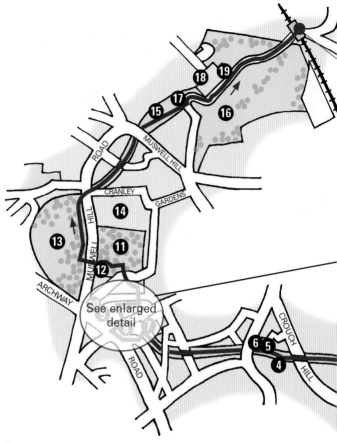

1 Finsbury Park
2 Finsbury Park Café
3 Start of Parkland Walk
4 Cape Adventure Playground
5 Spriggan Sculpture
6 Crouch End Station
7 Highgate Tunnels
8 The Boogaloo Pub
9 Highgate Tube Station
10 The Woodman Pub
11 Queen's Wood
12 Queen's Wood Café
13 Highgate Wood
14 Cranley Gardens
15 Muswell Hill
16 Alexandra Park
17 Grove Café
18 Alexandra Palace
19 Phoenix Bar & Kitchen

Places of Interest   Food & Drink

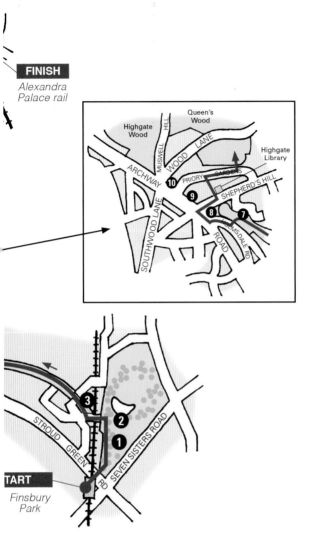

Queen's Wood

Highgate Wood

Highgate Library

MUSWELL HILL

WOOD LANE

ARCHWAY

PRIORY GARDENS

SHEPHERD'S HILL

SOUTHWOOD LANE

HELMSDALE RD

ROAD

10

9

8

7

STROUD GREEN

SEVEN SISTERS ROAD

3

2

1

WALK 11

Parkland Walk

PARKLAND WALK

Distance: 5 miles (8km)

Terrain: moderate, some steep hills

Duration: 2½ hours

Open: unrestricted

Start: Finsbury Park tube/rail

End: Alexandra Palace rail

Postcode: N4 2DH

The Parkland Walk is a 5-mile (8km) linear green footpath following a section of an old London train line. Closed since 1970, the London and North Eastern Railway (LNER) line ran between Finsbury Park and Alexandra Palace (via Stroud Green, Crouch Hill, Highgate and Muswell Hill). This walk follows the original bridges and cuttings of the line – you can still see 'ghost' stations along the route – although it bypasses the surface section of Highgate station and its adjoining tunnels, which are closed to walkers.

The walk opened in 1984 and is the city's longest Local Nature Reserve (LNR), supporting a wide variety of habitats and wildlife. Some 300 species of wild flowers have been recorded here and it's one of the few places in the capital where orchids rub shoulders with dandelions and ivy clambers up fig trees. Keep your eyes peeled for wildlife, including hedgehogs, foxes, bats, butterflies and a huge variety of birds – if you're lucky you may even spot a muntjac deer.

The Parkland Walk follows part of the Capital Ring walk, a 78-mile/126km route around London. Confusingly, it's divided into two sections: the longer southern section that runs between Highgate and Finsbury Park, and the northern segment linking Cranley Gardens with Muswell Hill. The overland detour, where the Highgate Tunnels interrupt the walk, is around one mile, depending on which route you take – we have chosen the most picturesque option via Queens and Highgate Woods. Our route continues beyond Muswell Hill to Alexandra Park, but if you prefer a shorter walk you can follow the southern section only (around 2 miles), which ends at Highgate tube station.

The Parkland Walk is an easy stroll in an urban environment. At times it can be quite busy – weekends attract walkers, dog walkers, joggers, runners and cyclists – while on weekdays you may even have the place all to yourself.

Start Walking…

Leaving Finsbury Park station, cross over Stroud Green Road and enter **Finsbury Park ❶** via the footpath to the left of Rowans Tenpin Bowl. Continue along the western edge of the park for around 500m (past the tennis courts) until you reach a junction. The path to the right leads to the lake (in the centre of the park) and **Finsbury Park Café 2** – a good place for a jolt of caffeine to get you moving. Here you turn left and leave the park over a colourful footbridge that crosses the East Coast Main Line (King's Cross to Scotland).

Finsbury Park

This 115-acre (46ha) public park – one of London's first grand Victorian parks – officially opened in 1869. It was one of the many 'people's parks', created to provide Londoners with open spaces as an antidote to the city's ever-increasing urbanisation and resultant pollution. Today, it's one of London's most diverse parks with a rich tapestry of landscapes, a mixture of open ground, formal gardens, avenues of mature trees and an arboretum containing rare trees.

The **Parkland Walk ❸** (South) starts on the right, just over the footbridge at the eastern end of Oxford Road, where the path rises on an embankment and overlooks the back gardens of Victorian houses. The route bridges Upper Tollington Park – where there's an avenue of London plane trees – and 600m further on you

cross Stapleton Hall Road, where the Gospel Oak to Barking rail line passes beneath the road (a concrete block is all that remains of an old signal post). Stroud Green station once stood here, with its platforms cantilevered out over the sides of the bridge over Stapleton Hall Road (from the bridge there's a fine view down the North London Line). The old station house still exists at road level, but there are no traces of the railway track or station buildings, which were destroyed in a fire in 1967.

The embankment gives way to a cutting as the land rises. The route continues beneath bridges carrying Mount Pleasant Villas,

Mount View Road and Crouch Hill. The Mount View Road bridge and Crouch Hill tunnels are particularly popular with graffiti artists, and the brickwork and abutments are covered in colourful artwork. Immediately after passing under Crouch Hill bridge, you pass the **Cape Adventure Playground** ❹ (a former electrical substation) on

Crouch End Station

the left. Past the playground the path enters Crouch Hill Park to the south of the old railway line. Innovative new school buildings here are home to Ashmount Primary School and Bowlers Community Nursery.

Highgate Tunnels

When you reach the end of the first section, before continuing take a little detour off the beaten track. Before exiting onto Holmesdale Road, head right at the end of the path and after around 100m you reach the old tunnels leading to Highgate Station. These are now blocked off and provide a perfect sanctuary for bats. Species in residence include long-eared, Natterer's and Daubenton's bats.

Food & Drink

❷ **Finsbury Park Café:** A lovely family-run café serving good coffee, breakfast fry-ups and a wide choice of lunch options (9am-5/6pm, £).

❿ **The Woodman:** A stylish gastropub near Highgate tube station with a huge beer garden, and a menu offering seasonal British cuisine (9am-10pm, 8pm Sundays, £).

⓬ **Queen's Wood Café:** This excellent community café is child- and dog-friendly, and serves home-cooked food with a good range of veggie options. It's highly-rated by both locals and visitors (10am-5pm weekdays, 9am-6pm weekends, £).

⓳ **The Phoenix Bar & Kitchen:** The Alexandra Palace restaurant offers freshly cooked, traditional menus, with a superb indoor area within the Palm Court and panoramic views over London from the terrace (11am-11pm, £).

Just before you reach the ghost station at Crouch End, look out for

Parkland Walk

the man-sized green **Spriggan Sculpture** ❺ by local artist Marilyn Collins. He embodies 'spirit of place' and nature's regenerative power and can be seen in one of the alcoves of the wall at the footbridge. The partly overgrown platforms are all that remain of **Crouch End Station** ❻, before the route passes under the site of the former station building and the road bridge over the cutting carrying Crouch End Hill. Beyond the cutting the view opens out on the northern side and skirts a hill, parallel to Hornsey Lane; there are many fine trees here, notably sycamore, oak and horse chestnut. The route bridges Stanhope Road on a footbridge and continues on an embankment to a brick-built bridge over Northwood Road.

The surrounding ground rises rapidly and the route becomes a cutting, at the end of which the portals of the southern pair of **Highgate Tunnels** ❼ (see box), also called the Holmsdale Road tunnels, come into view. The line to Alexandra Palace went through here and skirted around the back of Highgate Wood. The tunnels are closed to pedestrians and the southern section of the Parkland Walk ends here with an exit onto Holmsdale Road, which leads to Archway Road at **The Boogaloo** ❽ music bar. If you don't wish to continue to Alexandra Park, turn right and a few hundred metres along Archway Road is **Highgate**

Tube Station ❾, while a little further on is **The Woodman** 10 , a gastropub offering tasty food and good ales.

Queen's Wood

To pick up the northern section of the Parkland Walk to Alexandra Park, take the first right at the crossroads (past the Boogaloo) up Shepherd's Hill, and after a short distance turn left onto the narrow path alongside Highgate Library, signposted to Priory Gardens. Turn right at the end and walk along Priory Gardens for around 250m until, just before the road swings to the right, there's a pathway on the left (by no 10)

Queen's Wood Café

that leads into **Queen's Wood** ⓫ . Though not as well-known as neighbouring Highgate Wood (see box), Queen's Wood is wilder, with a greater variety of flora and fauna, and more structural diversity, and is probably a better reflection of the ancient woodland that once covered much of southern Britain. Spread over 51 acres (21ha), it features English oak and the occasional beech, providing a canopy above cherry, field maple, hazel, holly, hornbeam, midland hawthorn, mountain ash, lowland birch and the rare wild service tree.

The path through the wood joins the meandering Capital Ring (signposted) which runs north for around 100m before branching off to the left in an arc up and down the hilly woods, crossing over Queenswood Road before reaching **Queen's Wood Café** 12 , close to Muswell Hill Road. There's a lovely organic garden tucked away behind the café. Cross the road to enter **Highgate Wood** ⓭ through a small gate and walk along the eastern edge parallel with Muswell Hill Road. After around 500m you come to Cranley Gate in the northeast corner of the wood, where you exit

and cross Muswell Hill Road into **Cranley Gardens** ⓮ .

On the corner of Cranley Gardens you re-join the old railway track at Parkland Walk (North), which is well wooded with a mixture of hornbeam, sycamore, oak, birch, hawthorn and mature ash trees. The path dips in and out of wooded areas, with Muswell Hill on the left and expansive views over London to the right as you pass over the old 17-arch viaduct bridging St James's Lane. From here the silhouettes of Canary Wharf and the Shard can be seen on a clear day, and, through the trees, the transmitter mast at Crystal Palace. Around 200m further on you reach **Muswell Hill** ⓯ – a primary school now stands where the old station was – and a tunnel goes under the road to **Alexandra Park** ⓰ (see box), following the course of the old railway line which skirted round the western edge of the park. Continue straight ahead, passing the Little Dinosaurs play centre on your right and the **Grove Café** ⓱ a few hundred metres further on.

Around 200m after the café you come to a cross path with a car park on your right; turn right to connect with Alexander Palace Way, where **Alexandra Palace** ⓲ looms large on the left. The Grade II listed edifice – dubbed the 'People's Palace' and popularly referred to as 'Ally Pally' – was built by the Lucas Brothers, who also built the Royal Albert Hall around the same time. It was conceived to provide Victorians with a recreation centre within a green environment, and the

Alexandra Park

Named after Alexandra of Denmark, Princess of Wales and wife of Edward VII, this glorious 196-acre (79ha) public park was created in 1863 on the former Tottenham Wood Farm. The park is best known as the site of Alexandra Palace but has much more to offer, and is one of London's most beloved green spaces. Designed by Alexander McKenzie as a park and pleasure ground, it's a delightful mixture of informal woodland, open grassland, formal gardens and attractions. The vast, tree-lined slope offers gorgeous panoramic views over London – on a clear day it's even possible to see the Crystal Palace transmitter in southeast London (14 miles away)..

mighty Willis organ driven by two steam engines and vast bellows – it contained a concert hall, art galleries, museum, lecture hall, library, banqueting room and a theatre.

If you have time the palace is well worth a browse, while the **Phoenix Bar & Kitchen** 19 is a lovely place to sip a glass of wine and enjoy the views. If you're returning to Finsbury Park station by rail, Alexandra Palace station is a fairly easy downhill walk along the South Terrace – down a number of flights of steps – passing the Rose Garden on your left, via Bedford Road and a footbridge. From the station it's a seven-minute journey back to Finsbury Park.

original palace opened in 1873 but was destroyed by fire just 16 days later. With typically Victorian confidence, a new palace quickly rose from the ashes and opened on 1st May 1875, covering an area of some 7½ acres (3ha). Centred on the Great Hall – home to a

Alexandra Park

1 Pump House
2 Myddleton Square
3 Sadler's Wells Theatre
4 New River Head
5 Spa Green Garden
6 Owen's Field
7 Colebrooke Row
8 Islington Green
9 Astey's Row Rock Gardens
10 Greenpeace UK HQ
11 Canonbury Gardens
12 New River Walk
13 Canonbury Station
14 Petherton Road

Places of Interest   Food & Drink

FINISH
Manor House

START
Angel

PENTONVILLE RD.
CITY ROAD
UPPER STREET
ESSEX RD
CANONBURY ROAD
CANONBURY GR.
DOUGLAS RD.
ST PAUL'S ROAD
NEW NORTH ROAD

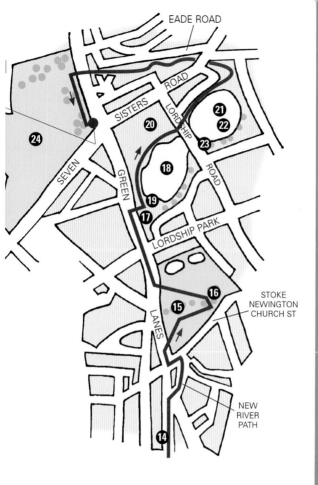

EADE ROAD

SISTERS ROAD

LORDSHIP ROAD

SEVEN

GREEN LANES

LORDSHIP PARK

STOKE NEWINGTON CHURCH ST

NEW RIVER PATH

WALK 12

- **15** Clissold Park
- **16** Clissold House Café
- **17** The Castle Climbing Centre
- **18** West Reservoir
- **19** West Reservoir Water Sports Centre

- **20** Woodberry Down Estate
- **22** East Reservoir
- **22** Woodberry Wetlands
- **23** The Coal House Café
- **24** Finsbury Park Café

New River Path

Distance: 5½ miles (8.8km)

Terrain: easy, mostly flat

Duration: 3 hours

Open: 8am to dusk or unrestricted

Start: Angel tube

End: Manor House tube

Postcode: N1 9LQ

The New River Path runs along the course of London's New River – not a river but an artificial (man-made) watercourse, and not especially 'new' either as it opened in 1613. James I put up half the cost of construction – the (then) huge sum of £18,500 – on condition that he received half the profits. The New River ran through his grounds at Theobalds Palace in Hertfordshire, and his involvement overcame opposition from local landowners to the scheme.

An impressive feat of engineering – masterminded by Sir Hugh Myddleton and surveyed by cartographer and mathematician Edward Wright – it was designed to bring water from springs at the River Lea in Hertfordshire to central London. Originally the river ended in Islington, just south of Sadler's Wells, but it now terminates at Stoke Newington. The aqueduct still supplies water today – up to 220 megalitres (48 million gallons) daily – accounting for some 8 per cent of London's daily water consumption. The motto of the New River Company was appropriately '*et plui super unam civitatem*' (and I rained upon one city).

The New River Path – developed between 1991 and 2003 at a cost of over £2m – is 28mi (45km) long, following the course of the New River from leafy Hertford to inner-city Islington. Wherever possible the route follows the historic water channel, but it also includes some open spaces and inner-city streets, and is waymarked throughout.

Our walk in Islington follows the 'heritage' section of the New River Path, starting at New River Head (see box right) in Islington and wending its way north through gardens and parks – and a few streets – before reaching the tranquil New River Walk, a charming linear landscaped park along the river's edge. The walk takes

A man of many talents, Sir Hugh Myddleton (1560-1631) was a cloth maker, mine-owner, goldsmith, banker, engineer and medieval entrepreneur. He was also royal jeweller to James I and MP for Denbigh Boroughs in Wales from 1603 to 1628. Myddleton was the driving force behind the ambitious construction of the New River, which brought clean water to London.

in lovely Clissold Park and the West and East Reservoirs in Stoke Newington, before concluding in Finsbury Park.

Start Walking…

Exiting Angel tube station, turn left along Islington High Street and right onto Pentonville Road. Some 200m on the left is Claremont Square (no public access). This is the site of the **Pump House ❶**, built in 1768 to house the steam engine used to pump water from the Round Pond near Sadler's Wells (New River Head) up to the Upper Pond, now the Claremont Square reservoir. Turn left into Mylne Street – named after William Chadwell Mylne, surveyor to the New River Company – past Claremont Square and continue past **Myddleton Square ❷** (and gardens) on your left, named after Sir Hugh Myddleton (see box).

The square's gardens contain many mature trees, seating and raised rose beds. Note the lovely façade of St Mark's church in the middle of the square. Continue to Myddleton Passage and follow the road round to Arlington Way (the Shakespeare's Head pub is on the corner) and **Sadler's Wells Theatre ❸**, where you turn right.

At the end of Arlington Way is the imposing **New River Head ❹** (see box) building on the right. Designed by Herbert Austen Hall, it was constructed in 1920 as the headquarters of the Metropolitan Water Board and became the HQ of Thames Water before it moved to Reading in 1993. It now houses luxury apartments but despite

New River Head

this, the New River Head remains an operational site. A pump here accesses the London Ring Main

New River Head

The termination point of the New River at New River Head in Islington was a small reservoir called the Round Pond, situated at an elevation suitable for water to be piped by gravity to houses in the City and surrounding areas. The circular basin was extended and a larger outer reservoir constructed in the early 1700s, and these became known as the 'Inner' and 'Outer' Ponds.

and a borehole brings up artesian water to help lower the water table under London. Just over Rosebery Avenue is **Spa Green Garden** ⑤ with a striking memorial to the Royal Flying Corps.

New River Tunnel

From St Peter's Street to Astey's Row the New River was confined in a tunnel, which crossed beneath Essex Road and resurfaced alongside what is today Colebrooke Row. When the Regent's Canal (see **Walk 7**) was built some 200 years later it had to pass underneath the New River, which it still does near the entrance to the Islington Tunnel.

We start our New River Path walk 'proper' here, heading north along Rosebery Avenue, left into St John Street and right into Owen Street past **Owen's Field** ⑥ – named after 16th-

New River Walk

century philanthropist Alice Owen – through which the New River once flowed. Leave the park and cross over Goswell Road and City Road into **Colebrooke Row** ⑦.

Here, a series of linear gardens run along the original route of the New River that flowed between Duncan Terrace and Colebrooke Row. Originally created in 1893, they form an important link in the series of green spaces along the former course of the river. Duncan Terrace Gardens have beautiful rose borders, tall herbaceous plants and lovely trees, including a tree of heaven with a cluster of 300 bird and bee boxes; part of the Secret Garden project, it's grandly entitled 'Spontaneous City in the Tree of Heaven'. The next section is Colebrook Row Gardens, which retains its shady wooded walk with lumps of tufa rock.

Continue to St Peter's Street and turn left towards the junction with Essex Road. Cross the road for a short diversion to **Islington Green** ⑧, where there's a fine contemporary war memorial by John Maine (2007) and a statue of Sir Hugh Myddleton by John Thomas unveiled in 1862 (at the far end of the green).

From here it's a walk north up Essex Road for some 500m until you pass the South Library, where you turn left up some steps to pick up the old route of the New River in a new linear garden, **Astey's Row Rock Gardens** ⑨ – there's a map of the river's course etched on the path. Around halfway along on the left

New River Walk

This magical watery park is one of the loveliest stretches of the entire New River Path: a tree-shaded walkway that meanders through landscaped gardens following the route of the river. After 100m or so, you pass an old circular stone hut, thought to have belonged to a watchman whose job was to prevent bathing and fishing in the New River. The narrow path wends its way to Willow Bridge Road (near the Marquess Tavern) where an old stone bridge leads over the watercourse. Further on there's an ornamental wooden bridge with a fountain on the right, and later a grander fountain in a large pool. The walk is landscaped with native English plants and specimen trees, including swamp cypress, dawn redwood and graceful weeping willows, and is a refuge for wildlife.

is the **Greenpeace UK HQ** 🔟, occupying a former laboratory building. The rockery walk opens out into **Canonbury Gardens** 1️⃣1️⃣, and once past the playground on the left, cross Canonbury Road (by the Myddleton Arms pub), to reach the first section of the walk to contain an actual watercourse – albeit restored and not the original river – called the **New River Walk** 1️⃣2️⃣ (8am to dusk – see box). It's accessed via a gate on the left at the start of Canonbury Grove and leads up to St Paul's Road (a distance of around half a mile).

At the end of the New River Walk, cross St Paul's Road into Wallace Road, passing **Canonbury Station** 1️⃣3️⃣ and the Snooty Fox public house. Keep straight ahead into charming **Petherton Road** 1️⃣4️⃣. The river once ran down the middle here, where its former course is marked by a path bordered by trees and grass. On the left the road is flanked by impressive 19th-century townhouses set back from the path, while on the right are former merchants' premises. After around 600m, Petherton Road meets Green Lanes, where the New River Path continues to the right of Green Lanes Methodist Church into Clissold Crescent. Turn left, past the New River Café, onto Stoke Newington Church Street. Opposite is delightful **Clissold Park** 1️⃣5️⃣, which you enter on the corner through the Robinson Crusoe Gate (near the pub of the same name). Head along the central path and turn right at the fountain in the direction of 18th-century (Grade II* listed) **Clissold House** 16, where there's an excellent café. The short stretch of water in front of the house was once part of the New River.

Clissold Park & House

Castle Climbing Centre

Head west to leave the park via
Lodge Gate, next to the park-
keeper's house, with the larger
(Beckmere) lake on your right.
Turn right along Green Lanes
and cross over the junction with
Lordship Park, and around 100m
further on you come to the **Castle
Climbing Centre 17** on your right.
Designed to resemble Stirling
Castle, it was originally a pumping
station built in 1854 by William
Chadwell Mylne to pump water
from the New River to northwest
London to fight a cholera
epidemic.

Cross Myddleton Avenue
and take an abrupt right into
the West Reservoir Centre,
where you're back on the New
River Path and the original New
River watercourse, which runs
along the western edge of Stoke
Newington's **West Reservoir 18**.
Stoke Newington East and West
Reservoirs were constructed
in 1833 to purify water from
the New River and provide
a water reserve. The West
Reservoir – where the
artesian water pumped out
at the New River Head was
released – is now used for
sports. The imposing **West
Reservoir Water Sports
Centre 19**, housed in the

West Reservoir Water Sports Centre

former '30s pump house, has a café and outdoor terrace.

The path along the West Reservoir is a pleasant wooded walk. Just before you reach the East Reservoir, there's a vast new housing development called **Woodberry Down Estate** ⓴ with a formal garden and impressive water features between the buildings and the path. The **East Reservoir** ㉑ is where the New River discharges and has been its southern 'mouth' since around 1946; water is stored here and piped to Walthamstow for treatment. The reservoir is now home to **Woodberry Wetlands** ㉒ (see box), opened to the public in 2016. (If you wish, you can walk around the reservoir and re-join the New River Path at its northern end.) On the East Reservoir side of Lordship Road is the original filter house, now the **Coal House Café** 23 , complete with a rooftop patio where you can watch the birdlife on the reservoir. Continuing along the western edge of the reservoir, the New River Path loops back on itself in a wide arc – crossing over Seven Sisters Road – where it's flanked by woodlands and fringed with grass verges on both sides. At the end of the path you pass through a kissing gate to Green Lanes and cross over to enter the northern section of **Finsbury Park** ㉔ .

This is where we end this walk, although the New River Path continues north on its merry way for another 22 miles (35km) to

Woodberry Wetlands

With 27acres/11ha of reed-fringed ponds and dykes, the wetlands (open 9am-4pm) are a haven for wildlife, including bats, insects (moths, butterflies, dragonflies, etc.), frogs, small mammals and a wealth of birdlife. The latter includes kingfishers, great-crested grebe, common tern and coot, plus wintering populations of pochard, shoveler, tufted and gadwall ducks, reed warbler and bunting, who migrate from Africa and spend the spring and summer here. Note that dogs aren't permitted in the reserve.

its source in the Lee Valley in Hertfordshire. To reach Manor House tube station, walk south down Green Lanes or take the more scenic route through the park.

Woodberry Wetlands

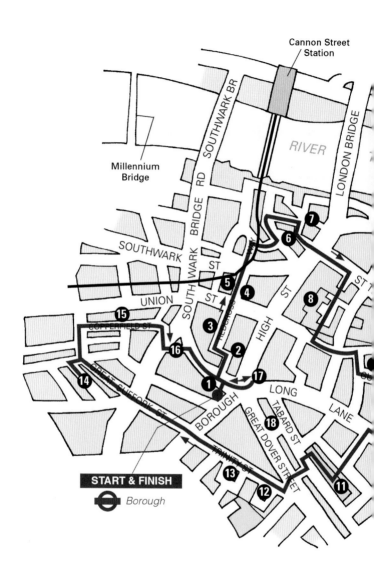

Cannon Street
Station

SOUTHWARK BR

RIVER

LONDON BRIDGE

Millennium
Bridge

SOUTHWARK
BRIDGE RD

ST

SOUTHWARK

UNION

SOUTHWARK ST

ST

⑤

④

HIGH ST

ⓞ⑥

⑦

ST T

⑧

⑮

COPPERFIELD ST

⑯

③

②

⑰

LONG

⑭

GREAT SUFFOLK ST

①

BOROUGH

TABARD ST

⑱

GREAT DOVER STREET

LANE

⑪

START & FINISH

Borough

TRINITY ST

⑬

⑫

THAMES

London Bridge
Station

T THOMAS ST

9

GUY ST

10

1   Joe's Kitchen

2   Little Dorrit Park

3   Red Cross Garden

4   Crossbones Garden of
      Remembrance

5   Boot & Flogger Wine Bar

6   Borough Market

7   Southwark Cathedral Gardens

8   Guy's Hospital

9   Guy Street Park

10   Leathermarket Gardens

11   Tabard Gardens

12   Merrick Square

13   Trinity Church Square

14   Drapers' Almshouses

15   All Hallows Churchyard

16   Mint Street Park

17   St George's Garden

18   Royal Oak Pub

● Places of Interest   ○ Food & Drink

WALK 13

Southwark
Gardens

SOUTHWARK GARDENS

Distance: 3½ miles (5.6km)
Terrain: easy, mostly flat
Duration: 2 hours
Open: 8am to dusk or unrestricted
Start/End: Borough tube
Postcode: SE1 1JX

S outhwark is one of the oldest and most fascinating parts of London, with a history dating back to Roman times, when it marked the easiest crossing point of the Thames; modern Southwark begins on the river, facing the City and Blackfriars. Just south of here archaeologists have found evidence of a prehistoric settlement, including burial mounds, while two major Roman roads converged in what is now Borough High Street. The Anglo Saxons gave Southwark its name, recorded in the *Domesday Book* of 1086 as Sudweca from the Old English *suth* and *weore*, meaning 'southern defensive work'.

Southwark gradually evolved into a centre for entertainment. During the Middle Ages it was London's 'red light' district, and hosted a famous annual fair. Being outside the control of the City, it attracted the criminal element, and Londoners visited for such 'amusements' as bull- and bear-baiting and to watch plays by Shakespeare and Christopher Marlowe at the Rose and Globe theatres. Less fortunate visitors ended up in one of Southwark's many jails, such as the infamous Clink.

What's striking about modern Southwark is how much of its history is still tangible. It has undergone a huge regeneration in recent times and is home to some ultra-modern buildings, including The Shard and City Hall, but still has a genuine feeling of age. There are reminders of the past around every corner; not just the magnificent Cathedral but also riverside warehouses, historic coaching inns and narrow, claustrophobic alleyways.

This corner of southeast London is also blessed with a wealth of small parks, gardens, squares, churchyards and other green spaces, which reflects the area's rich industrial, ecclesiastical, literary and medical history. Many were created in the 19th century to provide the poor with somewhere to enjoy green space and recreation facilities, and escape the city's pollution. Most of the gardens are open during daylight hours (unless shown otherwise) and many provide seating and wheelchair access.

Start Walking…

Leaving Borough tube station, turn left – passing **Joe's Kitchen 1**, a good place to grab a morning coffee – and cross Marshalsea Road to take the first right into Disney Place and right again for our first stop at **Little Dorrit Park 2**. Named after the character in Charles Dickens' novel of the same name, the small park contains flowerbeds plus a small peace garden and children's play area. Leave the park via the exit in the northwest corner onto Little Dorrit Court, which leads to Redcross Way, and cross over to see the charming **Red Cross Garden 3**, a short way up on the left. Originally laid out in 1887, the garden was part of a pioneering social housing scheme for the working classes conceived by Victorian philanthropist Octavia Hill (a co-founder of the National Trust). Recently restored to its former glory, complete with a pond, bridge and fountain,

Borough Market

First recorded in 1276, Borough Market (Wed-Thu 10am-5pm, Fri 10am-6pm, Sat 8am-5pm) is the largest wholesale and retail artisan food market in London, selling a vast range of produce from around the globe – everything from Argentine pastries to Spartan olive oil. Foodie heaven, it offers a huge choice of cafés, restaurants and street-food stalls (see http://boroughmarket.org.uk for information).

flowerbeds, serpentine paths, lawn and benches, it's the perfect frontage for the scheme's charming Tudorbethan-style cottages which were built in the 1880s.

Continuing along Redcross Way, cross Union Street to arrive at the poignant **Crossbones Garden of Remembrance 4**, a disused, post-medieval burial ground (see http://crossbones.org.uk). The site (noon-2pm

Red Cross Garden

weekdays) was an unconsecrated graveyard for 'single women' – a euphemism for prostitutes. They were known locally as 'Winchester Geese', because they were licensed by the Bishop of Winchester to work within the 'Liberty of the Clink' in Southwark, notorious for its brothels. The gates to the graveyard are decorated by a changing array of messages, ribbons, flowers and other tokens from visitors.

Southwark Cathedral

Past the garden on the left is the **Boot & Flogger** ❺, which looks like a pub and sounds like it should be a pub, but is actually a wine bar. Further along Redcross Way, our route takes us under a railway bridge and across Southwark Street to Park Street, where you turn right. Back under the railway, Park Street bears left to meet Stoney Street. Opposite is the splendid **Borough Market** 6 (see box), a wonderful place for

Food & Drink

❶ **Joe's Kitchen:** Situated near Borough tube station, this licensed café/restaurant is a good place for breakfast or lunch (7.30am-9pm, 9am weekends, £).

❻ **Borough Market:** Offers a wealth of places to have breakfast or lunch, or buy some takeaway food to eat in one of the gardens along the walk (10am-4-6pm, 8am Sat, £-££).

⑱ **The Royal Oak:** A lovely Victorian pub in Tabard Street, offering good ales (Harvey's) and tasty food (11am-11pm most days, £).

a mid-morning snack or indulgent lunch. Allow a good hour to browse the market, then turn right up Stoney Street and second right into Winchester Walk. At the end, cross Cathedral Street to enter **Southwark Cathedral Gardens** ❼.

The Cathedral gardens (8am to 6pm) provide a tranquil retreat from the surrounding urban landscape and are particularly popular with workers. Restored in 2001, the gardens occupy three sides of the magnificent 13th-century Southwark Cathedral, the

Leathermarket Gardens

In the South Churchyard of Southwark Cathedral there's an unusual granite boulder, which commemorates Mahomet Weyonomon. He was a Native American chieftain who came to London from Connecticut in 1735 to petition George II for restoration of his people's lands. Tragically, he and his companions died of smallpox before they managed to see the king.

oldest Gothic church in London. The East Churchyard herb garden was designed around the ruins of the medieval Lady Chapel, using herbs grown in the Apothecaries' Garden of St Thomas' Hospital (originally near the site), while the South Churchyard was designed using plants with Shakespearean and biblical connections.

Return to Cathedral Street, turn left towards the railway bridge and bear left into Bedale Street. Cross Borough High Street at the lights and continue down St Thomas Street, passing the Old Operating Theatre Museum and The Shard on your left. The entrance to the grounds of **Guy's Hospital** ❽ – founded in 1721 by Sir Thomas Guy – is on the right. The spacious forecourt leads through to a formal garden surrounded by a colonnade (similar to cloisters), beyond which lies one of King's

College London's campuses and a memorial garden to hospital staff lost in World War Two. (An alternative, step-free route is via Great Maze Pond and right into Collingwood Street.) Passing through the pleasant campus grounds you come out into Newcomen Street, where you turn left and continue into Snowsfields and right into Kipling Street for **Guy Street Park** ❾. Now a small urban park with a playground and flowerbeds, this was formerly a burial ground for Guy's Hospital. Leave the park to Weston Street (on the eastern side), cross over and enter **Leathermarket Gardens** ❿ on the left.

These lovely gardens were laid out in the '30s and take their name from the leather market and tanneries that thrived here in the 19th century. At the east end of the garden is a rectangular sunken area with formal beds, while the central area, separated by a low brick wall, has a raised circular rose garden surrounded by lawn with ornamental trees; behind here is a quiet garden planted with trees and grass, shielded by privet. Returning to Weston Street, turn left – passing the old

Guy's Hospital

leather market on your left (now workshops and a café) – and take a right at the crossroads down Long Lane and left into Staple Street. At the end of the street follow the path between Tabard House and Rochester House to **Tabard Gardens** 11, a large park set within the Tabard Gardens residential estate. The park encompasses large grassed areas, a wildlife area planted with shrubs and grasses, children's play area, outdoor gym, table tennis tables, artificial grass pitches and multi-use sports pitches.

Exit the gardens on the west side into Tabard Street, cross over and turn right into Becket Street and at the end cross over Great Dover Street and turn right at the Roebuck pub (on the corner) into Trinity Street. A short way along on the left is **Merrick Square** 12, a charming private garden square (no public access) laid out in the mid-19th century; it still has its original cast-iron railings and a variety of mature trees and shrubs. A little further along Trinity Street is **Trinity Church Square** 13, another private square. The church of Holy Trinity was built in

1824 and converted into a concert hall in 1975; called Henry Wood Hall, it's named after Sir Henry Joseph Wood who conducted the Proms for almost half a century. The Square was laid out between 1824 and 1832 and the gardens contain an imposing statue of Alfred the Great, late 14th-century in style and possibly one of a pair (with Edward the Black Prince) made for Carlton House garden in the 18th century.

The Drapers' Company

Founded in the 14th century on the wealth of the wool trade, the Drapers' Company was one of the 12 Great Livery Companies in the City of London. Like many Livery Companies, it provided a number of almshouses for the poor, including those in Glasshill Street built in 1820. The former almshouses are now privately owned and comprise a terrace of five houses with a communal front garden.

Continue along Trinity Street and cross over Borough High Street into Great Suffolk Street. After around 500m (past Southwark Bridge Road) you come to Pocock Street, where you turn left passing under two impressive railway arches to view the 'cottage-style' front garden of the attractive **Drapers' Almshouses** 14 (see box) on Glasshill Street. Return to Great Suffolk Street, turn left and take the second right into Copperfield Street, where halfway down on the left is **All Hallows Churchyard** 15. The grounds of former All Hallows Church (destroyed in

All Hallows Churchyard

World War Two) contain a lawn surrounded by flowerbeds and shrubberies, and a beautiful walled garden developed over 40 years with mature trees and plantings, draped in decades-old ivy that's a haven for wildlife. It's a unique natural habitat in the city, home to bats, squirrels, and resident birds, including wrens, robins, tits, blackbirds, magpies and wood pigeons.

At the end of Copperfield Street, over Southwark Bridge Road, is **Mint Street Park** 16. The park is very much focused on young people, with an adventure playground, a community stage, and a play area with a rock climbing wall and ball court. There are some gorgeous raised beds and tiered shrubbery planting, too. Leaving the park via the Marshalsea Road exit, turn right and cross over the road. Pass Borough tube station on your right and cross over Borough High Street to St George the Martyr church and **St George's Garden** 17 just behind it. The 18th-century church is often referred to as Little Dorrit's Church, as Dickens' character was baptised and married here; her kneeling figure can be seen in a stained glass east window. The churchyard was opened as a public garden in 1882, and the lovely peaceful walled garden has a fine display of flowers in spring under the huge London plane trees, beds planted with decorative box and a mixture of perennials. The northern boundary wall is an original wall of Marshalsea Prison (see box), indicated by a Historic Southwark plaque.

Marshalsea Prison

The infamous prison was in use from the 1370s and became notorious as a debtors' jail. Charles Dickens' father, John, was incarcerated here in 1824 for a debt to a baker, when Dickens was just 12 years old. Young Dickens was forced to leave school and work in a warehouse to support his family, which had a profound effect on the writer, who based several characters on his experience. Most notable was Amy Dorrit in the novel *Little Dorrit*, whose father is in Marshalsea for debts so complex that no one can fathom how to get him out.

This marks the end of the walk. Borough tube station, from where you started, is just opposite the church on the corner of Marshalsea Road and Borough High Street. If you fancy a drink after your walk, the **Royal Oak** 18 is a few minutes' walk south in Tabard Street.

1. *Cutty Sark*
2. Greenwich Pier
3. The Old Royal Naval College
4. National Maritime Museum
5. Statue of William IV
6. White House Café
7. Flamsteed House
8. Prime Meridian Line
9. General James Wolfe's Statue
10. Peter Harrison Planetarium

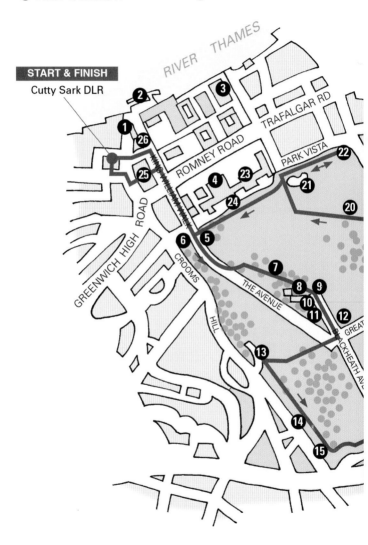

Places of Interest   Food & Drink

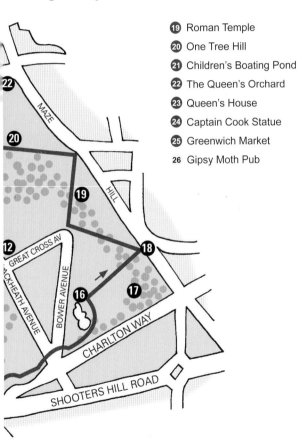

WALK 14

Greenwich Park

Distance: 4 miles (6.4km)
Terrain: moderate, some steep hills
Duration: 2 hours
Open: 6am to dusk
Start/End: Cutty Sark DLR
Postcode: SE10 8JA

G reenwich Park (Grade I listed) is London's oldest and most historic royal park, rich in magnificent buildings, museums, galleries, monuments, gardens and wildlife. It extends to 183 acres (73ha) – one of the largest green spaces in southeast London – and provides stunning views across the River Thames towards Docklands and the City. The park is part of the UNESCO Maritime Greenwich World Heritage Site, which provides a setting for several historic buildings, including the Old Royal Naval College, National Maritime Museum, Queen's House and Royal Observatory.

Open to the general public since 1830, Greenwich is London's oldest royal park. In fact, there has been a settlement here since Roman times, although Greenwich has 'only' been associated with royalty since 1427, when the land was inherited by Henry V's brother, the Duke of Gloucester, who built the Palace of Placentia in 1443 (long gone). It was the birthplace of Henry VIII and the park was one of his favourite hunting grounds. James I enclosed the park within brick walls – much of the original walls remain and define the park's modern boundary – and gave the park to his wife, Queen Anne. In 1675, Charles II chose Greenwich as the site for his Royal Observatory. The last monarch to use Greenwich was James II, whose daughter Mary donated the palace site as a hospital for sailors in the early 18th century. In 1873, the Royal Naval Hospital became the Royal Naval College (until 1998), and the National Maritime Museum was established in the park in 1934.

Set on a hill overlooking the Thames, Greenwich Park is an enticing mixture of green space, gardens and historical features. It's a Site of Metropolitan Importance for Nature Conservation and home to a wide variety of flora and fauna, including magnificent London planes,

oaks, alders and a splendid avenue of 400-year-old Spanish sweet chestnuts, plus flower, herb and orchard gardens. Our walk takes in many of Greenwich's best-known sites and visits all four corners of this beautiful park.

NOTE

If you're coming from central London, why not travel in style on a Thames Clipper ferry (see www.thamesclippers.com)? There are regular departures from the London Eye and various other piers.

Start Walking…

Leave Cutty Sark Dockland Light Railway (DLR) station, cross Greenwich Church Street and go east along College Way. A brief detour towards the river on your left brings you to the *Cutty Sark* ❶, one of the world's most famous sailing ships. She was first launched in 1869 and was a record-breaking tea clipper in her day – she has been fully restored after a devastating fire in 2007. Behind the *Cutty Sark* is **Greenwich Pier** ❷, where Thames ferry boats dock, while to the east is the **Old Royal Naval College** ❸ – designed by Sir Christopher Wren – the centrepiece of the Maritime Greenwich World Heritage Site (incorporating the Painted Hall and Chapel, among other buildings). Turn right down King William Walk past Greenwich Market on your right and the **National Maritime Museum** ❹ (see box) on the

left. You can easily spend a day exploring all the aforementioned sights, but you'll need to leave them for another day if you're to complete this walk (the museum alone warrants a day's exploration!).

At the end of King William Walk, enter Greenwich Park via St Mary's Gate, where there's a **Statue of William IV** ❺ off to the left and the **White House Café** ❻ on the right (in front of the Herb Garden). Continue along the main path – The Avenue – passing Conduit House on the right (near King George Street Gate), an 18th-century conduit head built to channel water to the new Naval Hospital. Just past the house take the path left, where the main path opens out, and climb the steep hill to **Flamsteed House** ❼. Designed by Sir Christopher Wren, it's the oldest of the observatory buildings, completed in 1676 and named after John Flamsteed (1646-1719), the first Astronomer Royal.

National Maritime Museum

The NMM was officially opened in 1937 and is the UK's leading maritime museum and the largest museum of its kind in the world. Its collections total over 2½ million items, from intricately carved ships' figureheads to the coat worn by Nelson (pictured) at the Battle of Trafalgar. (See www.rmg.co.uk/national-maritime-museum for information.)

Rose Garden & Ranger's House

The route takes you across the **Prime Meridian Line** ❽ which runs across the courtyard of the Royal Observatory, marking zero degrees longitude and Greenwich Mean Time (GMT). Walk round to the top of Blackheath Avenue to see the **Statue of General James Wolfe** ❾, commemorating his victory over the French in Quebec in 1759. Wolfe secured Canada for the British, but died in the battle (he's buried in St Alfege Church in Greenwich). The splendid views from here are renowned – it's one of the best viewpoints in London. Close by are the Royal Observatory Garden, the **Peter Harrison Planetarium** ❿ – fascinating for kids – and the main attraction, the **Royal Observatory Greenwich** ⑪ (see box), which also houses the Astronomy Café.

Walk south down Blackheath Avenue and you'll spot the **Pavilion Café** 12 on your left, housed in a charming 1906 octagonal building topped by a dovecote with a weather vane showing Nelson looking through his telescope. The café is fully licensed, with large gardens front and rear, and is an ideal place to have an alfresco drink or lunch. At the crossroads, turn right onto The Avenue and take the narrow path on the left and continue to the end towards Croom's Hill Gate; you pass an **Anglo Saxon Barrow Cemetery** ⑬ on your right – one of the oldest features in the park – dating back to the 6th century. When you reach McCartney House, turn left and walk south until, just past the tennis courts, you arrive at the handsome **Ranger's House** ⑭ (see box), opposite the semi-circular Rose Garden (best in June-July).

Royal Observatory Greenwich

One of the most important historic scientific sites in the world, the observatory is best known as the 'home' of Greenwich Mean Time (GMT) and the Prime Meridian, i.e. a line of longitude which is defined as 0°, established in 1851. Greenwich is the official starting point for each new day, year and millennium (at the stroke of midnight GMT, as measured from the Prime Meridian), adopted by international decree in 1884. Nowadays the Prime Meridian is marked by a powerful green laser that shines north across the night sky.

From the Ranger's House continue south, passing **Queen Caroline's Bath** ⑮ on the right; this odd little plunge pool is all that remains of Montague House which was home to Queen Caroline, the estranged wife of George IV, from 1798 to 1813. Follow the path around to the right, past Chesterfield Gate to

Ranger's House

Managed by English Heritage, Ranger's House is an elegant red-brick Georgian villa in the Palladian style. It dates from the early 1700s and was originally the official residence of the Ranger of Greenwich Park, when it was known as Chesterfield House. The property alone is worth visiting, but since 2002 it has housed the Wernher Collection: a wonderful assortment of jewels, paintings, porcelain, silver and more, amassed in the late 19th and early 20th centuries by German-born railway engineer's son, Sir Julius Wernher (1850-1912). It's an unusual collection of international importance, one of the best private collections of art assembled by one person, featuring some of Europe's most spectacular jewellery (see www.english-heritage.org.uk/visit/places/rangers-house-the-wernher-collection).

Blackheath Gate. Turning left along Blackheath Avenue, take the first path on the right just past the Lodge onto Bower Avenue, then right again to wend your way past the lake and the Wildlife Centre to the tranquil **Flower Garden** ⑯ north of the lake. Laid out in the 1890s, it's one of the horticultural showpieces of Greenwich Park, with splendid cedar, conifer, magnolia and tulip trees, fine lawns, and seasonal beds of spring and summer flowers. With its lake and deer park viewing areas, the Flower Garden is a favourite spot for parents with small children.

Just east of the garden, the path follows the edge of the **Wilderness Deer Park** ⑰ . Greenwich is the oldest of London's deer parks and has been home to red and fallow deer since it was enclosed in 1433. Today, two small herds of wild red and fallow deer live and breed in the wilderness and can be seen from several viewing points. This corner of the park is also a sanctuary for nesting birds, roosting bats (common pipistrelles), foxes, wood mice and many other species.

Continuing east with the Wilderness on your right, you arrive at the **Vanbrugh Park Gate** ⑱, named for John Vanbrugh, architect and dramatist, best known as the designer of Blenheim Palace and Castle Howard. His former home, Vanbrugh Castle and Park, is located further down Maze Hill on the corner of Westcombe Park Road (no access as it now houses some very exclusive private dwellings). From Vanbrugh Park Gate, head west towards the centre of the park and bear right at the cross paths onto Bower Avenue, where a short way up on the left are the remains of a **Roman Temple** 19 . Continue to Maze Hill Gate and follow the path along the edge of the park to the Maze Hill Gate House, where you turn left up the steep Cockpit Steps to **One Tree Hill** 20 . From this promontory there are fine views over the Old Royal Naval College and Greenwich, and further afield towards east and central London.

From One Tree Hill continue downhill to where the paths cross and head north (right) towards Park Gate Row; you'll spot the **Children's Boating Pond** 21 on the right. Turn right here to the north-eastern corner of the park – just inside the Creed Place Gate – and **The Queen's Orchard** 22 , created in the 17th century. Extending to ¾ acre (0.3ha), the orchard contains a variety of heritage fruit trees dating back to the 1500s, including apples, pears,

Food & Drink

6 **White House Café:** Located near St Mary's Gate, the café serves farm-made, dairy ice cream, milkshakes, cream scones, sandwiches and treats (9am-4/6pm, £).

11 **Astronomy Café:** Tucked away inside the Royal Observatory, the café has a sun terrace with panoramic views over Greenwich Park and serves a range of cakes, pastries and drinks (10am-4.30pm, £).

12 **Pavilion Café:** With large gardens to the front and rear, the park's licensed café is a nice place to sit in the sun with a drink, snack or lunch (9am-4/6pm, £).

26 **The Gipsy Moth:** Historic pub close to the *Cutty Sark*, with a large shady garden (10/11 am-11pm, £).

cherries, plums, peaches, apricot, nectarine, medlar and quince. It's open to the public on Sundays between Easter and October (1-4pm). Retrace your steps to Park Row Gate and continue west along the herbaceous border – at

Flower Garden

Wilderness Deer Park

200m, the longest in London – past the **Queen's House** ㉓ (see box) and Thomas Brock's **Statue of Captain Cook** ㉔. Cook (1728-79) was one of Britain's greatest seamen – explorer, navigator, cartographer and Royal Navy captain – and his statue is located (appropriately) in the grounds of the National Maritime Museum.

The path takes you back to St Mary's Gate where you entered the park. Retrace your steps along King William Walk and over Nelson Road, but this time take a 'short cut' through **Greenwich Market** ㉕ on the left – one of London's best covered markets – and exit on Durnford Street. *Cutty Sark* DLR station is off Creek Road just opposite – or you can take the Thames Clipper ferry from Greenwich Pier back to central London. If you fancy a drink before leaving Greenwich, why not try the historic **Gipsy Moth** 26 in Greenwich Church Street. A cosy traditional pub with a nice beer garden, it's named after Sir Francis Chichester's ketch (*Gipsy Moth IV*, which was once on display near the *Cutty Sark*), in which Chichester became the first person to sail single-handed around the world in 1966-67.

The Queen's House

This Grade I listed building is a former royal residence (originally part of Greenwich Palace) built between 1616 and 1619 for Queen Anne of Denmark (wife of James I), who died before it was completed. Designed by Inigo Jones, it was the first consciously classical building to be constructed in Britain and a landmark in British architectural history. Today, the house is part of the National Maritime Museum and serves as a gallery for some of the NMM's fine art collection, consisting of contemporary art, miniatures, oil paintings, photography, prints, drawings, watercolours and sculpture.

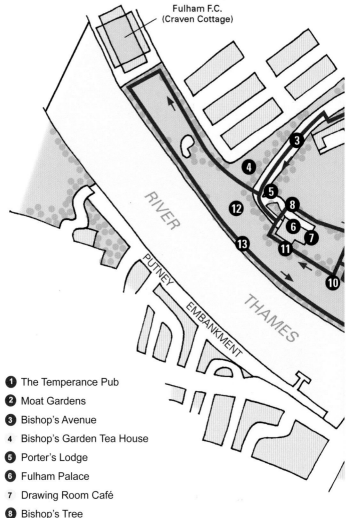

Fulham F.C.
(Craven Cottage)

RIVER

PUTNEY EMBANKMENT

THAMES

1 The Temperance Pub
2 Moat Gardens
3 Bishop's Avenue
4 Bishop's Garden Tea House
5 Porter's Lodge
6 Fulham Palace
7 Drawing Room Café
8 Bishop's Tree
9 Walled Garden
10 Holm Evergreen Oak
11 Tait Chapel
12 Bishop's Park
13 Thames Path

14 Pryor's Bank Gardens
15 All Saints Fulham
16 Almshouses
17 Putney Bridge
18 Fulham Railway Bridge

● Places of Interest   Food & Drink

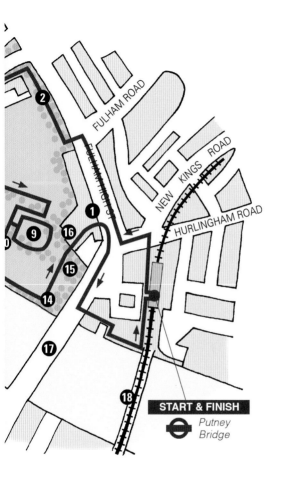

FULHAM ROAD

FULHAM HIGH ST

NEW KINGS ROAD

HURLINGHAM ROAD

①
②
⑨
⑯
⑮
⑭
⑰
⑱

START & FINISH

Putney
Bridge

Fulham Palace
Gardens &
Bishop's Park

Distance: 2½ miles (4km)

Terrain: easy, some steps and modest inclines

Duration: 1½ hours

Open: dawn to dusk

Start/End: Putney Bridge tube

Postcode: SW6 3UH

FULHAM PALACE GARDENS & BISHOP'S PARK

Fulham Palace Gardens in west London is something of a local secret; a delightful blend of history and horticulture in a tranquil riverside setting. The palace is one of London's oldest and most significant buildings, and was the country home of the Bishops of London for over 1,000 years. Excavations of the grounds have revealed several former buildings, including evidence of settlement dating back to Roman and Neolithic times.

The palace and gardens were once enclosed by the longest moat in England (and, quite possibly, Europe). It was around 1 mile (2km) in length and provided direct access to the River Thames. The moat was drained in the early '20s and only 13 acres (5.3ha) of the original 35 acres of palace grounds remain, but they provide the perfect picnic spot, with lawns, unusual tree species (including black American walnut, cork, Virginian oak and maples), and an 18th-century walled garden enclosing a knot garden, kitchen garden and pergola.

Fulham Palace Gardens has been celebrated since the days of Bishop Grindal (who served as bishop 1559-1570) – who is credited with introducing the tamarisk tree to Britain and reputedly sent grapes to Elizabeth I – but was made famous by Bishop Compton (1675-1713), a renowned botanist and plant collector who gave the gardens world significance. The grounds were landscaped by Bishop Terrick (1764-1777) during the rebuilding of the house, when the formal enclosed gardens were replaced with open lawns providing views to the river. The existing layout is mainly 19th century, with an earlier walled garden and some 18th-century landscaping. The gardens contain many rare trees, including an ancient evergreen holm oak that's around 500 years old.

Fulham Palace Gardens & Bishop's Park

Bishop's Park (Grade II listed) opened in 1893, on land that was originally part of the Palace Gardens. It offers something for everyone, including sports facilities, playgrounds, a café, ornamental lake and even a city beach. It also encompasses the beautiful Pryor's Bank Gardens to the south near Putney Bridge.

Start Walking…

Leaving Putney Bridge tube station, turn right and walk down the alleyway to New King's Road, turning left to Fulham High Street. Cross the road and turn right, passing the oddly named **Temperance ①** pub (a pub for teetotallers?) and continue for around 200m until, just past the junction with Fulham Road, you come to the entrance to Bishop's Park. This section of the park is called **Moat Gardens ②** and follows part of the course of the ancient moat around the original palace grounds. The area to the west – in between the Moat Gardens and the palace – was once the Warren, where the bishops hunted game, but is now occupied by Fulham Palace Meadows allotments.

Walk through the gardens, parallel with Fulham Palace Road, and exit through a gate at the end, turning left onto the path that runs alongside, and eventually joins, **Bishop's Avenue ③**. The 350m avenue is lined with mature plane trees, with tennis courts on the right and the All Saints' Primary and Moat schools on the left. You soon come to the early 20th-century iron gates and railings, which mark the entrance to Bishop's Park. The **Bishop's Garden Tea House ④** is on your right and the entrance to the grounds of Fulham Palace on your left.

Fulham Palace, West Courtyard

Enter the grounds crossing over the remains of the 15th-century

Fulham Palace

The palace (Grade I listed) has been a residence of the Bishops of London since around 700 AD. It was their country home from at least the 11th century and their main residence from the early 20th century until 1973 (when their residence was moved to Dean's Court, near St Paul's Cathedral). The current building consists of a Tudor manor house, dating from the reign of Henry VII (1485-1509) – said to be haunted by the ghosts of Protestant heretics who were persecuted in the great hall – with Georgian additions and a Victorian chapel. See www.fulhampalace.org for more information.

Fulham Palace, Walled Garden

Moat Bridge, through the old gateway, which has magnificent 19th-century gate piers, albeit with new (2012) wooden gates. To the left of the entrance is the quaint, early 19th-century Tudor-Gothic **Porter's Lodge 5**, while opposite is the late 19th-century Coachman's Lodge designed by William Butterfield. Continue straight ahead, passing some splendid trees, including Caucasian elm and horse chestnut, along the main path to **Fulham Palace 6** (see box). The entrance to the palace is through a Tudor archway, with huge medieval wooden gates, into the vine-clad Tudor West Courtyard – the oldest part of the palace – which has a central fountain on the site of the old well. From here you can visit

Fulham Palace, Terrace

the museum (free), chapel, great hall and café (etc.), dotted around the inner East Courtyard. The lovely **Drawing Room Café** 7 has a spacious terrace for sunny days.

From the courtyard return to the garden and turn right along the palace's outer wall, passing the **Bishop's Tree 8** on the north side of the palace. An unusual modern sculpture by Andrew Frost, it depicts some of the former bishops and their animals carved

---

Walled Garden

The restored 3.5 acre (1.4ha) walled garden (daily 10.15am-4.15pm, winter 3.45pm) includes a vegetable (kitchen) garden, vinery, fruit trees – including medlar, quince, apple, pear, plum and cherry, ranged along the paths and framed up walls – and a lovely knot garden replanted in its original 1830s design. The colour scheme of red, blue and yellow represents the colours of the coat of arms of Bishop Blomfield (1828-56) who's believed to have planted the original knot garden in 1831, which provides a colourful display in summer and early autumn. Also planted here is the complete range of Bishop Dahlias, named after various British bishops. The crowning glory of the knot garden is the spectacular wisteria pergola that encloses it. While visiting the garden look out for the charming market barrow, from where seasonal organic vegetables and fruit grown in the garden are sold, together with plants and fresh-cut flowers.

Thames Path

The Thames Path (www.nationaltrail.co.uk/thames-path) is a long-distance National Trail footpath running for 184 miles (296km) along the banks of the River Thames. From its source in the Cotswold Hills to the Thames Flood Barrier at Woolwich in southeast London, it passes through peaceful water meadows, unspoilt rural villages, historical towns and cities, before reaching the heart of London.

from the stump of a Cedar of Lebanon. At the rear of the palace the path leads to the expansive Great Lawn. Among the specimen trees scattered around the lawn are a Judas tree, damaged in the 1987 hurricane, a black walnut tree native to North America, an Atlas cedar from North Africa and an ancient sweet chestnut (you can purchase a guide book from the palace reception that identifies the garden's trees).

Follow the path round to the left to the **Walled Garden 9** (see box), heading right when you come to the bothies – old brick huts or rooms on the outer side of the walled garden – now restored and used by the current gardeners. After a few steps you reach the entrance to the garden via the impressive Tudor Gate; the coat of arms above the gate is that of Bishop Fitzjames (1506-22).

From the walled garden you can circle through the orchard and back to the lawn via the Tudor Gate. To the right of the gate is a maidenhair tree (ginkgo biloba) and some Tudor bee boles set into the wall; now blocked, they would have held traditional bee skeps (domed straw baskets). Over to the right is the garden's crowning glory, a magnificent **Holm Evergreen Oak 10** estimated to be around 500 years old (designated a 'Great Tree of London'), bent over and seemingly feeling its age. Continue along the path to the west of the palace (parallel to the Thames towpath) through the trees and turn right toward the palace, where you see the Tudor Revival **Tait Chapel 11** by William Butterfield, built onto the eastern façade of the palace in the 1860s (on the site of the medieval kitchens and service rooms). Along its wall are sprawling magnolias.

Holm Evergreen Oak

Follow the path around to the front of the palace, where on the right is a disabled car park, an education centre in the 19th-century stable block, and the site

Food & Drink

④ Bishops Garden Tea House: Housed in an Edwardian Pavilion (Grade II listed) and open seven days a week, the café offers healthy, locally-sourced produce and homemade dishes (9am-6.30pm, winter 4pm, £).

❼ Drawing Room Café: Licensed café in Fulham Palace open for breakfast, lunch and afternoon tea, serving soups, sandwiches, bangers and mash, cakes and cream teas (9.30am-5pm, 10am-4pm winter, £).

park hosts a farmers' market on Sundays (10am-2pm).

Opened in 1893, the park includes tennis courts, bowling greens, a clubhouse (sports pavilion), playgrounds, a lake and a unique urban beach. After entering the park turn right past the Bishop's Garden Tea House with bowling greens on your right and the playground on the left. Continue straight ahead and follow the right-hand path (parallel with Stevenage Road), with the beach and water play, ornamental lake and picnic areas on your left. Follow the shady path, past Fielder's Meadow and around the end of the park, to the **Thames Path** ⓭ (see box), which you follow back to Putney Bridge. (Adjacent to the northern end of the park is Fulham Football Club's ground, Craven Cottage.)

Continue along the lovely tree-lined Thames Path – the branches of the towering London plane trees almost touching the water – and admire the expansive views across the river. On the opposite bank, just before the cluster of boatyards and rowing clubs (and Putney Pier), are Leader's Gardens and the Putney Sculpture Trail. After passing the Bishop's Park playground the path runs alongside Bishop's Meadow, parallel to Fulham Palace. Around 200m before Putney Bridge there's a broad opening to **Pryor's Bank Gardens** ⓮, which was annexed to the park in 1894 (Pryor's Bank house

of the tithe barn (alas no more). Leaving the palace via the main gate, enter **Bishop's Park** ⓬ – the entrance is just to the left. The

Bishop's Park

was demolished in 1897) and remains a distinct garden within Bishop's Park.

The garden is divided into various sections, or mini-gardens. The first contains a memorial to local volunteers who died while serving in the International Brigade during the Spanish Civil War in 1936-39. It's followed by the rose garden with beautiful rising formal terraces, after which is a lawned area with an attractive mock Tudor pavilion, formerly a refreshments house. At the eastern end is the Sculpture Garden containing a fountain and modern statuary, including stone figures dating from the '40s, depicting Adoration, Protection, Grief and Leda, donated by sculptor James Wedgwood in commemoration of the coronation of Queen Elizabeth II. A further sculpture of a mother and child, Affection, by Joseph Hermon Cawthra, was added in 1963.

Behind the gardens a path leads into the churchyard of **All Saints Fulham** ⑮ (see box). On the north side of the churchyard in Church Gate are some attractive **Almshouses** ⑯ for 'twelve poor widows', founded and endowed in 1680 by Hereford MP and owner of nearby Munster House, Sir William Powell.

Exit Church Gate onto Fulham High Street, turn right and cross the road at the traffic lights. Continue to the right and go down the steps to the left of Putney Bridge Food & Wine and turn right to the Thames Path, where there's a majestic weeping willow. You're now facing **Putney Bridge** ⑰,

---

All Saints Fulham

The Kentish ragstone church tower is a local landmark dating back to 1440, while the rest of the church is Victorian, designed by Sir Arthur Blomfield in Gothic Perpendicular style. The interior contains many fine monuments from the old (pre-Victorian) church, including a number dating from the Civil War, while the churchyard contains the tombs of at least ten Bishops of London and the Fulham War Memorial.

---

designed by Sir Joseph Bazalgette – the man who built London's sewerage system – and built in 1884. It's the starting point for the annual Oxford-Cambridge University boat race, which ends at Chiswick Bridge. Follow the Thames Path east for around 200m until it bears left just before the attractive **Fulham Railway Bridge** ⑱ (also a pedestrian crossing). After 100m you reach Putney Bridge tube station, from where you started, and the end of the walk.

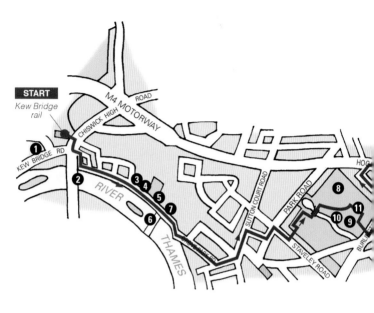

1. London Museum of Water & Steam
2. Kew Bridge
3. Bell and Crown Pub
4. Dutch House
5. City Barge Pub
6. Kew Railway Bridge
7. Bulls Head Pub
8. Chiswick House Gardens
9. Chiswick House
10. Ionic Temple
11. Chiswick House Café
12. Hogarth's House
13. Fuller's Brewery
14. St Nicholas Church
15. Chiswick Mall
16. Bedford House
17. Said House
18. Walpole House
19. Chiswick Eyot
20. Black Lion Pub
21. Linden House
22. Kelmscott House Museum
23. The Dove Pub
24. Furnivall Gardens
25. Hampshire Hog Pub
26. Ravenscourt Park
27. Walled Garden

● Places of Interest   ○ Food & Drink

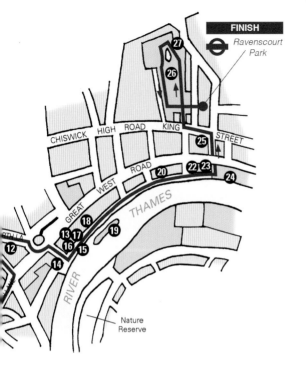

Chiswick House Gardens & Ravenscourt Park

Distance: 5mi (8km)

Terrain: moderate, some moderate inclines

Duration: 2½ hours

Open: dawn to dusk (or as noted)

Start: Kew Bridge rail

End: Ravenscourt Park tube

Postcode: TW8 0EF

The west London suburb of Chiswick sits on a meander of the River Thames, with Kew to the west and Hammersmith to the east. It's first mentioned in around 1,000AD as Ceswican, which is reputedly Old English for 'cheese farm' and may derive from the annual cheese fair held here until the 18th century (other etymologists claim that Chiswick means 'the village by the stony beach'). Until the early 19th century it was a rural outpost relying on agriculture and fishing, but increasing river pollution – blamed, in part, on the invention of the flush toilet – saw the fishing industry decline.

For a long time, rural Chiswick was a popular country retreat from London. Chiswick House was where the Earls of Burlington went to escape Piccadilly's summer heat. The area began to develop into a suburb of London in the late 1800s, and the population increased almost tenfold during the 19th century. It's an attractive and sought-after place to live, for its large houses (a mixture of Georgian, Victorian and Edwardian), wealth of green spaces and proximity to the Thames. It has also managed to retain its village atmosphere in places, not least along the riverbank, where it's hard to imagine central London is just a 30-minute train ride away.

Our walk takes you from Kew Bridge – along one of the loveliest stretches of the Thames – via Chiswick House and its lush gardens to Ravenscourt Park in Hammersmith, a 'secret' haven for people and wildlife, with a picturesque lake and charming walled garden.

Start Walking…

Leave Kew Bridge railway station and cross the road. If you turn back and look to your left you can see the tower of the **London Museum of Water & Steam** ❶, housed in a 19th-century riverside pumping station. Just past the traffic lights, bear left onto the quaintly named Strand-on-the-Green, which runs alongside the Thames and has some attractive 18th-century houses and good pubs fronting onto the river. To the right, at the beginning of the Strand, is elegant **Kew Bridge** ❷. There's been a bridge here since the mid-18th century; the current one, dating from 1903 and Grade II listed, is by Sir John Wolfe-Barry and Cuthbert Brereton.

> Modern Chiswick grew out of four villages which gradually merged to create the suburb you see today. One was Strand-on-the-Green; the others being Little Sutton to the east, Turnham Green to the northeast and Chiswick itself.

As you stroll along the riverbank, the surroundings feel semi-rural. On the left, a branch of Café Rouge with outside tables upstairs, provides an excellent vantage point for river watching.

Bell & Crown at high tide

Keep to the right where the Strand turns into a footpath, and you come to the first of several historic pubs: the **Bell and Crown** ❸ is a Fullers pub serving tasty food and a good selection of real ales. Smugglers used to land their contraband here but had to get their timing right as the river falls several metres at low tide, exposing a treacherous, muddy bed.

Just past the pub the river path narrows and the attractive villas lining it – including Prospect House with a curved frontage and balconies on the first and second floors – are separated from the water by just a shallow bank. A bit further on there's an attractive brick Georgian house (No 65) with a blue plaque to the painter Johan Zoffany (1733-1810) who lived here for 20 years from 1790 until

Strand-on-the-Green

his death. Soon after, you come to the eye-catching **Dutch House** ❹ , with gables and shutters in

building date from the late 15th century, although a World War Two bomb destroyed much of the original. The steel door and high window ledges reflect the fact that the river can rise a couple of feet up the pub's walls. The elegant pale green **Kew Railway Bridge** ❻ , opened in 1869, crosses the river at this point

Kew Railway Bridge

Eyot (Ait)

The word eyot (or ait) comes from the Old English for a small island, usually long and narrow, in a river or lake. The term particularly refers to islands in the Thames and its tributaries.

---

the Dutch style, painted in a striking blue and white split-diamond design. After passing a modern development, you see Tunnel Cottage (1752), a sprawling white house with a tunnel running beneath it to the riverside. As several warning signs confirm, the properties along the river path are at risk of flooding when the Thames rises at high tide – the price to be paid for living in this idyllic spot.

Further along is another recommended riverside pub, the slightly weather-beaten **City Barge** ❺ . Parts of the

and just beyond it is the last pub along this stretch of the river, the **Bulls Head** ❼ . Like many old pubs, it's attractively wonky, with low ceilings and creaking floorboards. Opposite is Oliver's Island, an eyot (see box) named after Oliver Cromwell who made his temporary headquarters at the inn during the Civil War. He's said to have taken refuge on the island, although this is unconfirmed.

A short way after the Bulls Head, a pink granite drinking fountain marks the end of the riverside walk and you turn slightly inland along Grove Park Road. At the roundabout, a white painted affair, veer left and take another left at the next junction (still on Grove Park Road) and left again over Grove Park Bridge, which

Chiswick House

Chiswick House

Chiswick House (Fri-Wed, Apr-Nov, 10am-5pm, entrance fee) was built in 1727-9 and is one of the finest examples of Palladian architecture in Britain. Its design echoes that of classical temples and was the result of collaboration between the 3rd Earl of Burlington (1694-1753) – who was inspired by the buildings he saw during his 'grand tours' of Italy – and architect William Kent (1685-1748). See http://chiswickhouseandgardens.org.uk for information.

framed by impressive entrance pillars and more sphinxes.

The 65 acres (26ha) of gardens – Grade I listed and restored in 2010 at a cost of £12 million – are of huge historical significance as the birthplace of the English Landscape Movement, i.e. the style of sweeping elegance which became the inspiration for splendid gardens, from Blenheim Palace to New York's Central Park. The gardens were originally intended to resemble those of ancient Rome, but were redesigned from the early 18th century in the geometrical style by Charles Bridgeman, to include

crosses the railway line. At the end of the bridge, cross Sutton Court Road to Lawford Road and at the end make a left along Park Road. After around 150m turn right into Staveley Road and after another 150m turn left (opposite Fitzroy Crescent) through a gated entrance into **Chiswick House Gardens 8** (7am-dusk).

Follow the main path straight ahead through the woods and fork left at the junction, with the cricket ground on your right. This leads to a graceful, balustraded stone bridge over the lake, from where you can see the rear of **Chiswick House 9** on the right. On the right is an **Ionic Temple 10**, while the path towards the house is lined with pillars displaying sphinxes and urns. At the rear of the house, you can turn left and go through an archway (Inigo Jones Gateway) to visit the award-winning **Chiswick House Café 11** – or turn right to the front of the house, which is

Chiswick House Gardens

ornamental buildings at the ends of vistas. Other parts of the gardens are in a more natural style, designed by Samuel Lapidge for the 5th Duke in 1784.

Many of the buildings were later demolished, but some remain, including the above-mentioned Ionic temple, a Doric column surmounted by a statue of Venus de Medici, three statues of Romans, two obelisks, the avenue of urns and sphinxes, a bridge,

Be sure to visit the Cascade, a tumbling waterfall that descends through a series of rocky steps and three archways, and the Raised Terrace, offering panoramic views of Kew Gardens across the river.

a deer house, a rustic house, a sunken Italian garden and a splendid conservatory (daily, 10am-3pm). The conservatory houses the oldest camellia collection in Britain (best in Feb-Mar). Today, the gardens offer a unique combination of stunning views, Italian follies, hidden pathways, dazzling flower displays, majestic ancient trees and, of course, a wealth of architectural delights.

Chiswick House Gardens, Cascade

Leave the gardens by the main entrance on Duke's Avenue, directly in front of Chiswick House – framed by magnificent Atlantic blue cedars of Lebanon, some almost 300 years old – and turn left along Burlington Lane. Just past the end of the gardens (opposite St Mary's Convent), turn left along Paxton Road, with its attractive, characterful terraced houses, which swings right into Sutherland Road. Turn right at the end into traffic-choked

Great West Road, an unexpected setting for another historic house. A short walk along Hogarth Lane (as the road was once known) is **Hogarth's House** ⑫ (Tue-Sun, noon-5pm, free), an attractive brick-built house used as a retreat by the artist William Hogarth from 1749 until his death in 1764. It opened as a museum in 1909, was damaged during World War Two and restored in 1997 for the tercentenary of Hogarth's birth. The nearby Hogarth Roundabout and Flyover are also named after the 'father of English painting' – a dubious honour!

Continue east along the Great West Road and cross the large roundabout via the underpass. Turn right along Church Street – Old Chiswick's 'high street' – which is more country town than urban highway. On the left as you enter the street is **Fuller's Brewery** ⑬ (tours can be booked); beer has been brewed in Chiswick for over 350 years, although the brewery dates from 1845. Near the end of Church Street, on the right, is an ancient right-of-way, Powell's Walk, and **St Nicholas Church** ⑭ (see box), where William Hogarth, fellow artist James McNeill Whistler (1834-1903) and architect William Kent (1685-1748) are buried.

Turn left at the end of Church Street onto **Chiswick Mall** ⑮, which runs along the Thames to Hammersmith. The Mall is lined with large, attractive, mainly 18th-century houses, some of which, unusually, are separated from their riverside gardens by a road; these include elegant **Bedford House** ⑯ –

Walpole House

former home of actor Sir Michael Redgrave – and, next door, **Said House 17**. Bedford House and nearby Eynham House were originally one property, dating from the mid-17th century, while Said House was the home of Sir Nigel Playfair, the actor-manager. Another fine house here is **Walpole House 18** – former home of Thomas Walpole, nephew of Britain's first Prime Minister Robert Walpole – a late 16th-century Tudor building altered in the 17th century and re-fronted in around 1730. The wrought iron railings and gate and the imposing porch with its ornamental Corinthian pilasters, are particularly noteworthy.

St Nicholas Church

The old village of Chiswick grew up around St Nicholas Church and along Church Street. St Nicholas is the patron saint of fishermen and sailors, among others, which is appropriate as Chiswick began life as a fishing village. The church was built in the Perpendicular style and its ragstone tower dates from 1446, although it's the only reminder of the medieval church; the rest was rebuilt in 1882 by John Loughborough Pearson, one of Britain's leading Victorian architects.

At the end of Chiswick Mall, the cottages of Durham Wharf screen the river from view and the mall becomes Hammersmith Terrace; No 7 is the former home of Emery Walker (1851-1933), engraver, photographer and printer. There's another eyot here, **Chiswick Eyot 19**, which can be reached on foot at low tide. Ahead, the road swings

left and reveals the **Black Lion 20** pub, allegedly haunted by the 'Hammersmith ghost', a 19th-century spectre.

Pick up the Thames-side path again in front of the pub. Just past the Upper Mall Open Space, there's another handsome historic pub, The Old Ship, dating from 1722. There's a short stretch of modern housing before you reach **Linden House 21** at number 60 Upper Mall. Built in 1733, it's a grand brick building with an entrance flanked by Ionic columns, home to the London Corinthian Sailing Club (founded 1894) since 1963. Further along at No 26 is **Kelmscott House Museum 22** (see box), a handsome Georgian building where artist, designer and man-for-all-seasons William Morris lived from 1879 until his death in 1896.

A bit further along is **The Dove 23**, which used to be a coffee house but is now the quintessential English pub; it claims to have the smallest bar in England and its riverside terrace is a coveted place from which to watch the University Boat Race (in late March). Charles II and Nell Gwyn apparently had assignations

Kelmscott House

William Morris' last London home was built in around 1780 and originally called The Retreat. Morris renamed it after his Oxfordshire home, Kelmscott Manor, and occasionally travelled between the two homes by boat – those were the days! In 1891, Morris established the Kelmscott Press at 26 Upper Mall. Today, the William Morris Society occupies the basement, where there's a small but interesting museum (Thu and Sat, 2-5pm) with a collection of Morris designs and memorabilia.

at the Dove, and it has inspired writers and musicians. In 1740, the poet James Thomson wrote *Rule, Britannia!* in an upstairs room, while Gustav Holst used to compose music at the pub – it must be something in the beer!

It's time to leave the river and head towards Ravenscourt Park. Just past the Dove the path leads to **Furnivall Gardens** 24 – once the location of the mouth of Hammersmith Creek – where you turn left and follow the path along the gardens' edge and take the subway under the Great West Road to Cromwell Avenue (via a footpath). At the end of the avenue turn left into King Street, passing the outstanding **Hampshire Hog** 25 gastropub, and around

200m on the right is the entrance to **Ravenscourt Park** 26 , down Ravenscourt Avenue and under a railway arch.

This beautiful 33-acre (13ha) public park was established in 1888, designed by JJ Sexby on land surrounding Ravenscourt House (the house was destroyed by German bombs in 1941). The origins of the park lie in the medieval manor and estate of Palingswick (or Paddenswick), first recorded in the 12th century, when it was owned by the Bishop of London. An earlier manor house was rebuilt in 1650 and in 1747 it was sold to Thomas Corbett (1687-1751), Secretary to the Admiralty, who renamed it Ravenscourt. This is probably derived from the raven in Corbett's coat of arms, which was itself a pun on his name – *corbeau* is French for raven.

Ravenscourt Park combines attractive landscaping with a range of wildlife habitats. Its crowning glory is the enchanting **Walled Garden** 27 , secreted in the northeast corner of the park. To reach it, follow the main path for around 400m passing the bowling green and café on your right. At the end of the path bear slightly right and go through the gates

Ravenscourt Park

into the garden. Originally part of the manor's kitchen garden, it's laid out in a traditional Victorian symmetrical design with rose beds and arches, and exotic herbaceous beds featuring yuccas, giant poppies, irises and gunnera. It's bordered below the wall with shrubs, while scented plants such as lavender and honeysuckle make it a treat for the nose as well as the eyes. The garden is a wonderful, Zen-like retreat, with benches and bowers.

Ravenscourt Park, Walled Garden

Leaving the walled garden turn right and follow the path round past the children's playground and take the path on the left to the lake. Continue past the lake and walk along the right edge of the park on a woodchip path passing another playground and a huge paddling pool. When you reach the main entrance arch, go straight ahead down an alleyway past the tennis courts on the left, turn right at the end and go under the railway line to Ravenscourt Park tube station on your left –

and the end of the walk. If you fancy lunch or a pint, there's a wide choice in the area, including the delightful **Hampshire Hog** 25 gastropub in King Street that you passed earlier.

Food & Drink

5 The City Barge:
Welcoming pub with well-kept real ales, good food and plenty of outdoor space (noon-11pm/midnight, from 10am weekends, £).

11 Chiswick House Café:
This lovely award-winning café and terrace in Chiswick Gardens offers a British seasonal menu using produce from the kitchen garden (8.30am-4/6pm, £).

25 The Hampshire Hog:
A lovely gastropub – airy and light – close to Ravenscourt Park, offering superb (free range and organic) food, with a pretty beer garden (10am-11pm, closes 6pm Sun, £).

● Picnics: You can picnic in both Chiswick House Gardens – where specific areas are set aside – and Ravenscourt Park.

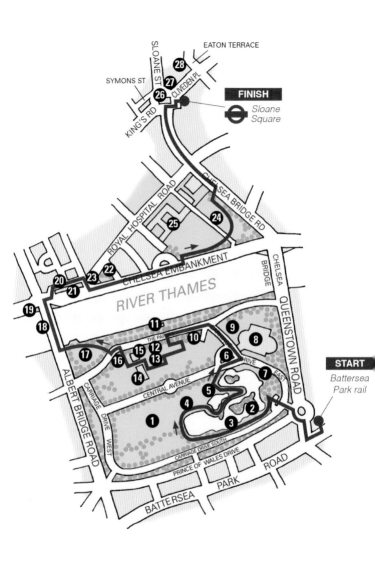

WALK 17

Battersea Park & Chelsea Gardens

Distance: 4mi (6.4km)

Terrain: moderate, some gentle hills

Duration: 2 hours

Open: Battersea Park 8am to dusk (others as noted)

Start: Battersea Park rail

End: Sloane Square tube

Postcode: SW8 4BL

Opened in 1858 by Queen Victoria, Battersea Park is a delightful 200-acre (83ha) public park on the south bank of the River Thames opposite Chelsea. It's one of inner London's largest, most interesting and varied parks – a cornucopia of delights – a lovely place to escape the crowds and enjoy nature at any time of year. You could easily spend a whole day in Battersea Park, which retains many typically Victorian features, including a serpentine carriage drive, a formal avenue, an irregular lake, various flower gardens and shrubberies, and a wealth of magnificent specimen trees. It's spectacular in autumn when the trees are a riot of colour.

In 1951 the park was a venue for the Festival of Britain, when an area of 37 acres (15ha) was transformed into the Festival Pleasure Gardens – the funfair remained an attraction until 1974. The Festival Gardens comprised a Grand Vista – an exquisitely framed view redolent of English country parks – plus upper and lower terraces linked by wide flights of steps to the Fountain Lake, flanked by willows. A flower garden formed the central part of the gardens, which also contained an amphitheatre, while to the east was an aviary and children's zoo. Many of these features have been restored, including the stunning Vista Fountains, whose 50 jets form a beautiful focal point.

Today, the park is home to a small aviary, boating lake, bandstand and several all-weather outdoor sporting facilities, including 19 tennis courts, a sports centre (with gym and running track), zip-lining/rope course and soccer pitches. It also boasts an events/conference centre (Battersea Evolution), the Pump

Battersea Park & Chelsea Gardens

House Gallery, Battersea Park Children's Zoo and two cafés.

From Battersea Park our walk continues over Albert Bridge to Chelsea and along the Thames and Chelsea Embankment, taking in the Chelsea Physic Garden, Ranelagh Gardens and the Royal Hospital, Chelsea, before terminating in Sloane Square.

The park covers an area once known as Battersea Fields. On 21st March 1829, the Duke of Wellington and the Earl of Winchilsea met on the Fields to settle a matter of honour, although neither actually attempted to shoot the other and Winchilsea later made a grovelling apology.

Boating Lake

Start Walking…

Leaving Battersea Park railway station, turn right along Battersea Park Road for 50m to the traffic lights and right again into Queenstown Road to Queen's Circus. Continue around the Circus anticlockwise and the entrance to **Battersea Park ❶** is the second left via the Rosery Gate. Cross over the main driveway, skirting Rosery Gardens, and turn left along the south side of the 16-acre (7ha) **Boating Lake ❷**, a popular nesting spot for waterfowl, herons and swans. After 200m you come to Barbara Hepworth's statue **Single Form ❸**, a huge bronze over 10ft (3m) high. A typical Hepworth 'bottle-opener', it's a memorial to her friend Dag Hammarskjold, the UN Secretary General who died in a plane crash in 1961.

Continue along the wooded path around the western end of the lake – passing the sub-

Three Standing Figures

tropical gardens, which have some majestic oak, ash and palm trees – to discover another of the park's impressive sculptures, **Three Standing Figures ❹** by Henry Moore. The 7ft (2.1m) stone statue – depicting three standing women, draped in flowing garments – was created in 1947 and has been situated in the park since 1950. Follow the lakeside path to the right of the Ladies Pond and cross over a rustic wooden bridge dating from the '20s; the path meanders around the edge of the lake and brings you back to the handsome Italianate **Pump House Gallery ❺** (Wed-Sun, 11am-4pm). It's housed in a four-storey water tower (Grade II listed), built in 1861 to supply water to the lake and cascades, and has been a gallery since 1999, hosting a year-round programme of contemporary visual arts exhibitions.

Leaving the gallery, turn right, where a short distance along on the left is the striking **XXIV Division Memorial** ⑥ by Eric Kennington (1924). It commemorates the 24th East Surrey Infantry Division, which served on the Western Front in World War One, where it suffered over 35,000 men killed, wounded or missing. Turning left onto Carriage Drive East you pass the Australian Memorial Garden, where there's a memorial to the 5,397 Australian aircrew lost in action over Europe during World War Two. If you're peckish head back to the eastern end of the lake and the **Pear Tree Café** ⑦ , a favourite spot for all-day alfresco dining.

Turning right at the end of the path (after the Australian Memorial Garden) brings you back to the main Carriage Drive, on the other side of which is the **Millennium Arena** ⑧ , a vast indoor sports centre opened in 2000. Walk north (with the Arena on your right) to reach the **Thrive Battersea Main Garden** ⑨ . Thrive (www. thrive.org.uk) is a charity that employs gardening to bring about positive changes in the lives of people living with disabilities or ill

> ### Festival of Britain Pleasure Gardens
>
> In 1951 the northern section of the park (as far as Carriage Drive East) was transformed into the 37-acre (15ha) 'Pleasure Gardens' as part of the Festival of Britain celebrating the centenary of the Great Exhibition of 1851. The Fountain Lake, Grand Vista and Russell Page Garden have been restored and have a nostalgic '50s character, with the original bold blue and orange colours still evident.

health, or those who are isolated, disadvantaged or vulnerable; the charity is responsible for maintaining many of the park's beautiful gardens.

At the top of the drive turn left past the entrance to Battersea Evolution (a purpose-built events and conference centre), Pier Point Café (mixed reviews) and public toilets, to reach the **Children's Zoo** ⑩ . Residents include lemurs, meerkats, monkeys, Shetland ponies and pygmy goats and there's a fee to visit (10am-4.30/5.30pm). Just past the zoo on the right is the striking **Peace Pagoda** ⑪ , a gift from the Nipponzan Myōhōji Order of Japanese Buddhist monks, installed in 1985 on the Thames embankment.

Directly opposite the Pagoda is the lovely **Russell Page**

Fountain Lake

Food & Drink

(7) Pear Tree Café: Situated alongside the lake in Battersea Park, the Pear Tree conjures up delicious dishes using seasonal produce, which you can enjoy while watching the ducks and boats (daily 8am-5pm, £).

(27) Côte Brasserie: Modern, all-day French brasserie (chain) in Sloane Square, serving regional specialities and traditional classics (7am-11pm, £).

(28) The Antelope: Traditional pub in Eaton Terrace (No 22) a stone's throw from Sloane Square, with wood-panelling, etched windows, stripped floors and a classic English menu. (noon-11pm, £-££).

Garden **(12)**, with beautiful formal flowerbeds (lots of roses), box hedges and lawned areas. To the right of the garden is the **Tea Terrace Kiosk (13)** and just beyond it the magnificent **Fountain Lake (14)** – the fountain springs into action around once an hour – overlooking the **Grand Vista (15)**, created for the 1951 Festival of Britain Pleasure Gardens (see box).

To the left of the Grand Vista is the charming **Old English Garden (16)**, originally created in 1912; neglected for years, it's gained a new lease of life in recent years thanks to Thrive (see above). The intimate walled garden is a riot of colour and fragrance (with jasmine, mint, roses and violets) in spring and summer, with dwarf box hedges, pergolas, a pond with goldfish and lilies, and plenty of seating to encourage quiet contemplation.

Albert Bridge

Albert Bridge used to be nicknamed 'The Trembling Lady' due to its tendency to vibrate when large numbers of people walked over it – signs at the entrances warn 'troops must break step when marching over this bridge'!

Leaving the garden by the north entrance, cross over Carriage Drive North and take the diagonal path left that runs past the **Herb Garden (17)** – which contains an interesting collection of culinary and medicinal herbs – to the river. Turn left (west) to exit the park onto Albert Bridge Road, taking in the expansive view of **Albert Bridge (18)**. Designed by Rowland Mason Ordish and opened in 1873, it was originally a toll bridge; the tolls were unsuccessful and were scrapped after six years, although the tollbooths remain in

Chelsea Physic Garden

The 3½ acre (1.4ha) garden is a historic, living museum as well as a haven of beauty and relaxation, with a lovely café (Tangerine Dream). It was founded in 1673 and is London's oldest botanical garden and Britain's second-oldest after the one at the University of Oxford (1621). But unlike almost all of the other gardens in this book, there's a hefty entrance fee (which varies by season), which must also be paid even to access the café. The entrance is in Swan Walk.

place and are the only surviving examples in London. The bridge looks particularly stunning at night, when it's illuminated.

Over the bridge is Chelsea Embankment and **Albert Bridge Gardens** ⑲, a small public park containing benches, lawns, shrubs and flowerbeds. Turn right off the bridge and walk east along the Embankment passing **Cheyne Walk** ⑳, a stylish historic street that takes its name from William Lord Cheyne (1657-1728), who owned the manor of Chelsea until 1712. Most of the houses here were built in the early 17th and 18th centuries when they fronted the Thames, long before the Embankment was constructed in the 19th century.

Facing Cheyne Walk alongside the Embankment is **Chelsea Embankment Gardens** ㉑, which consist of two strips of land either side of Albert Bridge. The two gardens comprise ornamental bedding, paths and seating, with shrubbery backing Cheyne Walk, each containing a number of statues. Just past the gardens is Royal Hospital Road, leading to the **Chelsea Physic Garden** ㉒ (see box), a botanical garden founded in 1671. Adjacent to the Physic Garden – just past Royal Hospital Road – is striking **Old Swan House** ㉓ (No 17 Chelsea Embankment), built in 1876 by Richard Norman Shaw, said to be the finest Queen Anne Revival domestic building in London.

Continuing along the Embankment (with the Physic Garden on the left) you pass handsome terraces of red brick and terracotta mansion apartments, until around 150m beyond Embankment Gardens (road) is the entrance to **Ranelagh Gardens** ㉔ (10am-dusk). Turn right, circling the South Ground where the Chelsea Flower Show takes place in May. These lush gardens extend to 52 acres (21ha), including the grounds of the **Royal Hospital, Chelsea** ㉕ (see box), and feature many mature trees, flowerbeds and grassy areas, with secluded and shady walks. In the 18th century they were the site of the famous Ranelagh Pleasure Ground, although Wren's formal Royal Hospital gardens were swept away between 1850 and 1868. The current Ranelagh Gardens

Chelsea Embankment

date from around 1860, when the Chelsea Embankment was built.

Leave Ranelagh Gardens in the northeast corner onto Chelsea Bridge Road, turn left and continue straight ahead at the junction with Royal Hospital Road and on to Lower Sloane Street and **Sloane Square** 26 – both named after Sir Hans Sloane (1660-1753), whose private collection was the foundation of the British Museum. In the early '80s the Square lent its name to the 'Sloane Rangers', the young, often snooty and ostentatiously well-off members of the upper classes. Today, it's famous as the site of Peter Jones department store and the Royal Court Theatre. If you fancy a drink or something to eat, the Square offers a wealth of choices, including the inexpensive **Côte Brasserie** 27 , an all-day French café/restaurant at 7-12 Sloane Square. If you prefer a traditional pub, **The Antelope** 28 at 22 Eaton Terrace is just a few minutes away.

This marks the end of our walk – Sloane Square tube station is located in the southeast corner of the square.

Royal Hospital, Chelsea

The Royal Hospital, now a military retirement home, was founded in 1682 by Charles II for veteran soldiers and designed by Sir Christopher Wren. It's built around three courtyards, the central one opening to the south, the side courtyards to the east and west. The building remains almost unchanged from Wren's original, except for minor alterations by Robert Adam between 1765 and 1782, and the stables, which were added by Sir John Soane in 1814. Today, the hospital is home to some 300 Chelsea Pensioners, who receive board, lodging, nursing care and a distinctive red uniform. However, much of the site is open to visitors, including the great hall, octagon, chapel, courtyards and grounds. There's also a small museum dedicated to the hospital's history. See www.chelsea-pensioners.co.uk for more information.

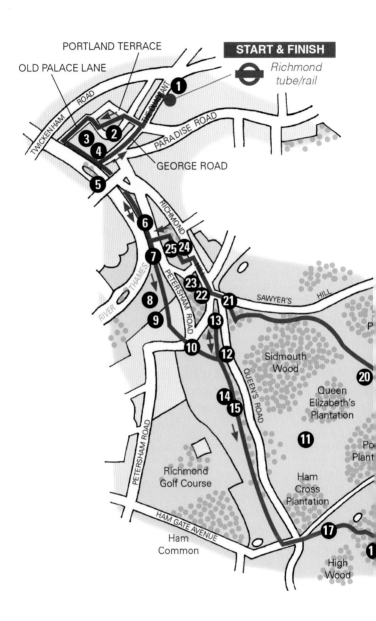

START & FINISH

Richmond
tube/rail

PORTLAND TERRACE

OLD PALACE LANE

TWICKENHAM ROAD

PARADISE ROAD

GEORGE ROAD

RICHMOND

RIVER THAMES

PETERSHAM ROAD

RICHMOND HILL

SAWYER'S HILL

Sidmouth
Wood

Queen
Elizabeth's
Plantation

QUEEN'S ROAD

PETERSHAM ROAD

Richmond
Golf Course

HAM GATE AVENUE

Ham
Common

Ham
Cross
Plantation

High
Wood

Places of Interest   Food & Drink

1 Butter Beans Café
2 Richmond Green
3 Richmond Palace
4 White Cross Pub
5 Richmond Bridge
6 Bingham Hotel & Restaurant
7 Buccleuch Gardens
8 Petersham Meadows
9 Petersham Nurseries
10 Petersham Gate
11 Richmond Park
12 King Henry's Mound
13 Poet's Corner
14 Pembroke Lodge
15 Butler's Pantry Café
16 Isabella Plantation
17 Bottom Gate
18 Broomfield Hill Gate
19 Pen Ponds
20 Leg of Mutton Pond
21 Richmond Gate
22 Royal Star & Garter Home
23 Petersham Hotel
24 Terrace Gardens
25 Hollyhock Café

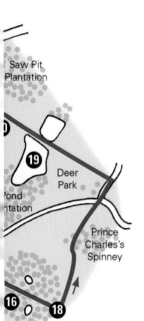

Saw Pit
Plantation

Deer
Park

Pond
ntation

Prince
Charles's
Spinney

16   18

Richmond Park

Distance: Distance: 7½mi (12km) or 4½mi (7¼km) – see below

Terrain: moderate, some steep hills

Duration: 4 hours (2 hours)

Open: unrestricted

Start/End: Richmond tube/rail, 371 or 65 bus to Petersham Gate

Postcode: TW9 1DN

RICHMOND PARK

Richmond Park is the largest royal park in London and the second-largest urban park in Europe, extending to 2,360 acres (955ha). Its royal connections date back to Edward I (1272-1307), who established a palace at the manor of Shene (Sheen). In the late 15th century Henry VII rebuilt Sheen and renamed it Richmond Palace after his lands in Yorkshire. In 1625, Charles I brought his court to Richmond to escape the plague in London and turned part of the land into a park for hunting deer; he also enclosed it within a high brick wall extending some 8 miles (13km) in length. The park remained in royal ownership until 1851.

Richmond Park is classified as a European Special Area of Conservation, a National Nature Reserve and a Site of Special Scientific Interest, with a plethora of flora and fauna. The oldest, largest and most widespread inhabitants of the park – its trees and, especially, its oaks – provide homes for a wide range of wildlife, from ants and beetles to birds and bats. However, the most ubiquitous residents are the red and fallow deer (numbering around 650), which roam freely within much of the park. It's also an important refuge for squirrels, rabbits, foxes, shrews, mice, voles, cardinal click and stag beetles, plus numerous varieties of fungi. Birdlife is hugely varied, with some 150 species recorded (over 60 breed here), including all three native woodpeckers, kestrels, owls and a variety of waterfowl.

The park has changed little over the centuries, despite the surrounding urbanisation and its proximity to London. Cars are only permitted entry during daylight hours and no commercial vehicles apart from taxis are allowed. Pedestrians and cyclists have

24-hour access, except when there's a deer cull (usually in November), and the park also has designated bridleways and cycle paths. It offers a wide range of amenities for visitors, including formal and informal gardens, playgrounds, kiting, bike hire, guided walks, stables, fishing, golf, two cafés and various refreshment points. See www.royalparks.org.uk/parks/richmond-park for more information.

> **NOTE**
>
> As in other royal parks, the use of barbecues and the lighting of fires are prohibited, as is the playing of radios or other musical equipment. Dog owners are urged to keep their pets on a lead, both for the safety of the park's wildlife and that of the dogs (a number have been killed by deer).

Start Walking…

The walk begins at Richmond station, but before you start, you need to decide whether you want a 'long' or a 'short' walk: by taking the 371 or 65 bus to Petersham Gate (10) you can save 1½mi/2.4km (each way) – or you can enjoy the walk through the town and along the riverside. If you need a coffee to perk you up, **Butter Beans** 1 just outside the station is a good choice. If you opt for the longer route, cross the road outside the station and go down Old Station Passage, then turn left on Little Green. After around 100m you come to Little Green (the actual green, not the road), where you take the diagonal path across the grass to Portland Terrace and **Richmond Green** 2.

Covering some 12 acres (4.8ha), Richmond Green was described by architectural authority Nikolaus Pevsner as 'one of the most beautiful urban greens surviving anywhere in England'. A popular cricket venue, it consists mainly of open grassland bordered by mature trees and surrounded by fine old houses. Cross the green diagonally, heading west, to reach Old Palace Yard and the Grade I listed remains of **Richmond Palace** 3 – previously Sheen Palace, occupied by Henry VII, Henry VIII, Elizabeth I and Charles I. The palace was largely demolished after the execution of Charles I in 1649, but a few strikingly handsome buildings remain, including the Wardrobe, Trumpeters' House and the Gate House (1501).

Richmond riverfront

Walk 18

From Richmond Green, follow the signs to the river, which take you down Old Palace Lane to the Thames towpath – on your right is Richmond Railway Bridge and,

Richmond Bridge

just beyond that, Twickenham Bridge. Turn left to follow the riverside walk – named Cholmondeley Walk after the Earl of Cholmondeley – reputedly the first public footpath in England. After a few hundred metres you come to the **White Cross** ❹, a historic Young's pub with a riverside terrace, situated just before Water Lane (where there's a slipway). At certain times of the year the towpath can flood; in the 18th century there were two paths: a wet path for tradesmen and a dry path for gentle folk.

Continue along the towpath (Buccleuch Passage), past some grass terraces and boat houses to **Richmond Bridge** ❺, a handsome 18th-century (Grade I listed) stone arch bridge, and the oldest surviving bridge across the Thames in London. Follow the path under Bridge Street, where it's lined with attractive gardens and mature trees. There are a number of pubs and restaurants

fronting the river here, including the Gaucho restaurant – with a gigantic London Plane tree (38m/125ft) – and the Georgian **Bingham Hotel & Restaurant** ❻, which has a lovely terrace.

Just past the Bingham you pass the Richmond Canoe Club and arrive at **Buccleuch Gardens** ❼ – a popular picnic spot – with the larger Terrace Gardens on your left. At the end of the gardens go through a scissor gate, turn left and cross **Petersham Meadows** ❽, which exits onto Church Lane; to the right is the celebrated **Petersham Nurseries** ❾ and its delightful café. Continue straight ahead and just before St Peter's Church take the footpath to the

Pembroke Lodge

Once a humble mole-catcher's cottage, the lodge was enlarged in 1788, renamed Hill Lodge, and given by George III to the Countess of Pembroke (with whom he was besotted). Further expansion in the late 18th century by Sir John Soane and Henry Holland resulted substantially in the elegant building you see today.

left, passing the Ranelagh Harriers Clubhouse and, round to the right, the chic Dysart Petersham gastropub. At the end of the path, cross Petersham Road to **Petersham Gate** ⑩ and enter Richmond Park.

Richmond Park ⑪ covers a vast area, but our walk takes in just a few of its highlights! Just after entering the park take the diagonal (secondary) path on the left, which takes you to **King Henry's Mound** ⑫, a prehistoric burial mound (probably Bronze Age) encircled by holly bushes. This is the spot where King Henry VIII allegedly stood in 1536 to watch a rocket fired from the Tower of London to signal that his wife Anne Boleyn had been executed for treason and he was free to marry Lady Jane Seymour. The mound offers fabulous views of the Thames Valley to Windsor Castle in the west and an astonishing distant view of St Paul's Cathedral to the east (there's a free telescope to help you admire the view).

Just 200m north of the mound (via the John Beer Laburnum Walk) is **Poet's Corner** ⑬, where there's a bench dedicated to the memory of pop star Ian Dury (1942-2000) – famous for hits such as *Hit Me with Your Rhythm Stick* – who used to come here with his family. The central bench is inscribed with the words *Reasons to Be Cheerful*, the title of another Dury song, and incorporates a plate with a QR barcode which, when scanned with a mobile phone, allows you to hear some of his songs. A few

Isabella Plantation

Packed with exotic plants, the plantation is a magical garden for all seasons, very different from the subdued landscape in most of the rest of the park. It contains three ponds – the Still Pond, Peg's Pond and Thomson's Pond – and a 500m stream flows through it, colonised by ferns, water plantains and brooklime. The plantation is home to the national collection of 50 Kurume evergreen azaleas (introduced to the west from Japan in the '20s by the plant collector E. H. Wilson), which line the ponds and streams – at their best in late April and early May – and large collections of rhododendrons and camellias, plus many other rare and unusual trees and shrubs.

metres away is Poet's Seat, a curved metal bench where there are some inscribed lines by the Scottish poet James Thompson (1700-1748), famous for writing the words to *Rule, Britannia!*

St Paul's Cathedral from King Henry's Mound

From King Henry's Mound head south – passing a thatched cottage with a lovely rose garden and arbour – and follow the path to Grade II listed **Pembroke Lodge** ⑭ (see box), set in 13 acres (5ha) of landscaped grounds. It's a popular wedding venue and houses the **Butler's Pantry 15** , a restaurant/café with a large terrace offering wonderful views.

Continue south via the splendid Hornbeam Walk (on the path running parallel to Queen's Road) to Ham Cross, then head over the road and take the path due east signposted for the **Isabella Plantation 16** (see box) and enter the Plantation via the **Bottom Gate 17**. This stunning ornamental woodland garden – extending to 42 acres (17ha) – was created by George Thomson (the park superintendent) after World War Two, and opened to the public in 1953.

Isabella Plantation

Leave the plantation via the main **Broomfield Hill Gate 18** and continue to your left passing Corretts Copse, Gibbet Wood and Prince Charles's Spinney on your right. You soon arrive at a main intersection with the road from Robin Hood Gate, where a short distance away there's a car park and a café. Just past the car park take the main path to the left to **Pen Ponds 19** – probably

Food & Drink

1 Butter Beans: Just outside Richmond station, Butter Beans serves good coffee and tasty food (7.30am-5pm, 8/9am weekends, £).

6 Bingham Hotel & Restaurant: If you want to treat yourself to a superb lunch, the acclaimed Bingham is highly recommended (020-8940 0902, lunch noon-2.30pm, Sun 12.30-7pm, ££).

15 Butler's Pantry: Pembroke Lodge tearooms offer a wide variety of refreshments including hot lunches (with a Sunday roast) and cream teas (9am-5.30pm, £).

25 Hollyhock Café: A lovely café in Terrace Gardens, with the bonus of panoramic views (dawn-dusk, £).

named after former deer pens – some 400m north in the middle of Beverley Brook. Created in 1746, the ponds are actually a lake divided in two (the upper and lower ponds) by a causeway; they're an excellent place to observe wildfowl and fishing is also allowed here (permits are available from Holly Lodge in the north of the park). There are around 30 ponds in the park, many of which were created to drain the land or provide water for livestock.

From Pen Ponds, continue northwest on the main path passing the **Leg of Mutton Pond** 20 and Queen Elizabeth's Plantation on the left. After another few hundred metres you skirt Sidmouth Wood on the left and soon after the path runs parallel to Sawyers Hill to **Richmond Gate** 21, where you exit the park.

Directly opposite the gate is the imposing **Royal Star & Garter Home** 22, built for disabled military veterans and opened in 1916 (it now houses luxury apartments). From here you can take a 371 bus back to Richmond station. If you prefer to walk, head down Richmond Hill opposite, passing Wick House on the right, former home of painter Joshua Reynolds, and Nightingale Lane on the left leading to the outstanding **Petersham Hotel** 23. A little further on the footpath widens and some 100m on the left are steps leading down to the beautiful **Terrace Gardens** 24, which are on a steep slope offering spectacular views over the Thames. The gardens contain many unusual trees, including redwood, maidenhair, spruce and cedars, along with a rose garden, flowerbeds and a herbaceous border.

Follow the main path through the gardens, past the exemplary **Hollyhock Café** 25, and exit onto

Petersham Road and cross to the Thames towpath. Retrace your original route along the towpath back to Richmond station, making a short-cut just before the **White Cross** 4 pub via Water Lane and George Street.

Arcadian Thames

In the 18th century an Arcadia ('idyllic pastoral landscape') was re-created along the Thames below Richmond Hill. Magnificent royal and aristocratic palaces were constructed – such as Doughty House, which was for sale in 2017 for £100 million! – along with gardens and parks linked by a series of avenues, set within a framework of meadow and woodland. The Thames Landscape Strategy (http://thames-landscape-strategy.org.uk) aims to conserve this special stretch of river and enhance its character.

1. Wimbledon Common
2. Light on the Common Café/ Restaurant
3. Rushmere Pond
4. Cannizaro Park
5. Hotel du Vin & Bistro Wimbledon
6. Millennium Fountain
7. 'Gothick' Aviary
8. Bust of Haile Selassie
9. Keir Garden
10. Statue of Diana
11. Italian Garden
12. Azalea Dell
13. Lady Jane's Wood
14. Belvedere
15. The Retreat
16. Sunken Garden
17. Herb Garden
18. Fox & Grapes Pub

Places of Interest   Food & Drink

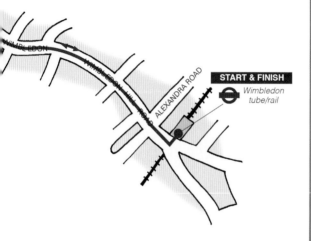

START & FINISH
Wimbledon
tube/rail

ALEXANDRA ROAD

WIMBLEDON HILL ROAD

WIMBLEDON

Cannizaro Park

WALK 19

Distance: 3½mi (5.6km)
Terrain: moderate, some hills
Duration: 1½-2 hours
Open: 8am to dusk (9am weekends)
Start/End: Wimbledon tube/rail
Postcode: SW19 7NL

CANNIZARO PARK

Lovely Cannizaro Park is a Grade II* listed park on the edge of Wimbledon Common. A private garden for some 300 years before opening to the public in 1949, this 'secret' garden combines immense natural beauty with a unique collection of rare and exquisite trees and shrubs, including sassafras, camellia, rhododendron and other heather-family plants. The 35-acre (14ha) park has a large variety of green areas, from expansive lawns and leisurely walks through woodlands, to formal areas such as the Sunken Garden next to Cannizaro House and the Italian Garden near the pond.

The park has its origins in the 299-acre (121ha) Warren Estate on the southern edge of Wimbledon Common. It was purchased in 1705 by William Browne, a wealthy London merchant, who built Warren House (which later became Cannizaro House) in the early 1700s. The name Cannizaro dates from 1832 when Count St Antonio leased the house. He later succeeded to the dukedom of Cannizzaro in Sicily and left England to live with his mistress in Milan, but his long-suffering Scottish wife Sophia remained in the UK and retained her title as Duchess of Cannizzaro. When she died in 1841 the estate was recorded under her name and, apart from the loss of a 'z', the name has stuck ever since.

The greatest contribution to today's park was made by Mr and Mrs Kenneth Wilson – and their gardeners George Dillistone and Richard Allison – who lived on the estate from 1920 to 1947 and designed a new garden, much of which remains today. The Wilsons' daughter, Hilary, married the 5th Earl of Munster in 1928 and 20 years later, after her parents' death, sold the entire estate to Wimbledon Corporation and Surrey County Council for £40,000. Cannizaro House is now home to the Hotel du Vin & Bistro Wimbledon, a luxury hotel and restaurant.

There's something to see in Cannizaro Park at any time of the year, as it features a superb display of seasonal flowers, shrubs and trees. Early in the year there are snowdrops and crocuses, followed by camellias. Then come daffodils and bluebells in spring, along with rhododendrons, azaleas and magnolias. In summer, the Rose Garden is intoxicating and there's a spectacular display in the Sunken Garden, while in autumn maples and other trees provide a riot of colour.

Start Walking…

Exit from Wimbledon station, and take a right turn onto Wimbledon Hill Road. From here it's a stroll of around ¾ mile (1.2km) – around 15 minutes – to reach Wimbledon Common. If you'd rather conserve your energy for the park, you can take the no. 93 bus to the village from outside the station, alighting opposite the Rose and Crown on the corner of the High Street, from where the park is a 10-minute walk. The village is one of Greater London's most desirable

Wimbledon Common

Wimbledon Common, together with Putney Heath and Putney Lower Common, is the largest expanse of heathland (1,136 acres/460ha) in London. Created in 1871 by an Act of Parliament for public recreation and the preservation of flora and fauna, the common provides an oasis of calm in the midst of urban southwest London. The common is a popular recreational area, not least for walkers, runners, cyclists and horse riders (with 16mi/26km of bridleways), plus an 18-hole golf course (and two golf clubs), cricket pitches and 48 acres (20ha) of playing fields.

residential areas and features a cornucopia of chic shops, cafés and bars, set amongst handsome period buildings and open spaces. The walk from the station takes you over a mini roundabout and left at another until you reach the Rose and Crown pub on your right. Here you turn left into the High Street – yes, Wimbledon has two high streets for the price of one! The High Street leads to Southside Common and the corner of **Wimbledon Common** ❶ (see box). If you fancy a coffee or breakfast before getting started,

Cannizaro House & Sunken Garden

Walk 19

Cannizaro House

William Browne built Warren House – later Cannizaro House – in the early 1700s. Former residents of the house and estate included Thomas Walker, a friend of Britain's first Prime Minister, Sir Robert Walpole; John Lyde-Brown, Governor of the Bank of England; and Henry Dundas, 1st Viscount Melville (1742-1811), Home Secretary under Prime Minister William Pitt the Younger. Henry Dundas lived there from 1785-1806, when the house was a major social centre for royalty and senior politicians. In later years, visitors included Lord Tennyson, Oscar Wilde and Henry James. Sensitively refurbished to its former glory, the house is now a luxury hotel, with a bistro restaurant and an orangerie overlooking the gardens.

Light on the Common 2 at number 48 is an excellent choice.

From here it's a pleasant 10-minute walk across the eastern corner of the common, following the path that runs south of **Rushmere Pond** 3, after which you cross over Cannizaro Road to West Side Common. The entrance to **Cannizaro Park** 4 is just ahead, to the right of the **Hotel du Vin & Bistro Wimbledon** 5 – which has a lovely restaurant – in the former Cannizaro House (see box).

Enter the park via the wrought-iron gates – bearing the monogram 'EKW' (for Mr and Mrs E. Kenneth Wilson, the last owners) – to the right of the hotel entrance, and just ahead is the **Millennium Fountain** 6. The work of Richard Rome, this patinated bronze fountain in the shape of a multi-spouted teapot was installed in 2001. Follow the path round to the right to the white decorative **'Gothick' Aviary** 7 – housing a colony of multi-coloured canaries and zebra finch – built by the park's staff in 1976 and reputedly modelled on Pisa cathedral. A bit further on past the holly grove you pass the 'tennis court garden' (the site of the former tennis court) on the left, containing a collection of ornamental trees and shrubs and a **Bust of Haile Selassie** 8, the last Ethiopian emperor, by Hilda Seligman. In 1936 Selassie was a guest of Sir Richard Seligman and his sculptor wife Hilda in Wimbledon during his exile from Ethiopia (1936-1941).

Around 50m further on, through an avenue of trees in the northeast corner of the park, the path leads to **Keir Garden** 9 (see box). Inside the triangular, partially-walled area is Keir Cottage (set into the wall adjoining Camp Road) and a 19th-century chapel. The area to the south of Keir Garden is a carpet of crocuses

Millennium Fountain

in February, while just past the garden on the right is a lovely rose garden. Continue west for around 100m along the main path to the northwest corner of the park, where there's a striking 19th-century **Statue of Diana** ⑩ with a fawn.

The Keir

A neighbouring property, the Keir, was bought by E. Kenneth Wilson in around 1932. The house was converted into flats but the gardener's cottage and the 1.2-acre walled garden were added to the grounds of Cannizaro.

Return to the main Maple Avenue (planted between 1920 and 1930), which runs southwest through woodland and grass clearings for around 200m, where it joins up with the main tarmac path from the house. Turn to the left – there are some artists' studios in the old potting sheds on the right – towards the pond. From the southeast corner of the pond (sheltered by oaks), Yorkstone steps lead up to the west lawn, where the path leads back to the

house. Immediately south of the pond is the gate to the walled garden, formerly the kitchen garden and now a grass picnic area with gravel paths; note the olive trees in the northeast corner and a Chinese glory tree in the northwest corner. From the walled garden you enter the magical **Italian Garden** ⑪, enclosed within low brick walls topped with a stone balustrade. The garden contains a wood and brick arbour covered in climbing roses and wisteria, some splendid specimen trees and lovely decorative urns. Look for the beautiful Japanese silk trees at the entrance.

Surprisingly, the Italian Garden was only created in 1970s, although it seems much older. The garden has been restored in recent years by The Friends of Cannizaro Park (see box), including the picnic benches and tables. Steps at the southern end of the garden lead through another gate to the Wild Garden, a green dell with rhododendrons, azaleas, magnolias, acers, primroses, a lovely snow-drop tree and majestic oaks. To the right is the rustic Water Garden, along the banks of a hidden stream, a tributary of Beverley Brook that runs across Wimbledon Common. From here you head west to the **Azalea Dell** ⑫ and **Lady Jane's Wood** ⑬, which were largely developed by the Wilsons at the same time as the Maple Avenue, and boast stunning displays of rhododendrons and azaleas in spring. The wood was planted by Henry Dundas Viscount Melville

Maple Avenue

to celebrate his wedding to Lady Jane Hope in 1793.

A number of paths lead southeast from Lady Jane's Wood through the Mediterranean Garden up to rising ground surmounted by the **Belvedere** ⑭ , around 300m south of the house. Built in the late '70s, the Belvedere is a folly comprising a high retaining wall topped by stone balustrades, supporting a rectangular platform decorated with eight free-standing columns – not unlike a small Greek temple. From here there are panoramic views across the park and the surrounding common. From the Belvedere take the secondary path that leads southeast to a small spur of land planted out in the early '90s with ornamental trees and shrubs, called **The Retreat** ⑮ . Retrace your steps along the park's border (lined by houses on the edge of the park) across the magnificent

The park has a long history of staging arts, sculpture and musical events, including the Wimbledon Cannizaro Park Festival in summer (held intermittently).

② Light on the Common: A cosy café/restaurant in Wimbledon Village, open for breakfast, lunch and dinner (8am-10/10.30pm, 9am weekends, closes 3.30pm Sundays, £).

⑤ Hotel du Vin & Bistro Wimbledon: The elegant hotel and restaurant occupying the former Cannizaro House is a splendid venue for coffee, lunch or afternoon tea in the Orangerie or on the terrace overlooking the park (0330-024 0706, lunch 12.30-2.30pm, Sunday noon-4pm, ££).

⑱ The Fox & Grapes: Located just outside Cannizaro Park, this outstanding gastropub in Camp Road is a popular place for lunch, particularly the Sunday roasts (8.30am-11pm, see www.foxandgrapeswimbledon.co.uk for kitchen times, £-££).

west lawn to the south of the house.

From the portico of the balcony on the south side of the house, a flight of shallow stone steps lead down to the spectacular **Sunken Garden** 16 , the centre laid to grass decorated with geometric flowerbeds, with benches and paved walks flanked by beds with seasonal plants including English roses, tulips, asters, lavender, impatiens, petunias and marigolds. A path that runs around the perimeter of the Sunken Garden leads through a wrought-iron gate in the southeast corner, to the enchanting bijou **Herb Garden** 17 , recently planted with olive trees beyond the thyme beds, an appropriate place to end the visit to Cannizaro Park.

Head back to the front of the hotel. If you fancy a drink or lunch you have two great choices, the hotel restaurant 5 (the fixed menu is good value) or the **Fox & Grapes** 18 gastropub just a few minutes away, north of the

park in Camp Road. To return to Wimbledon station, simply retrace your steps across the common to Wimbledon Village and back to the station.

The Friends of Cannizaro Park

A registered charity, the Friends are volunteers who work tirelessly to maintain and improve the park for the benefit of visitors and the community as a whole, ensuring that the park remains a jewel in Wimbledon's crown, a haven for wildlife and an enduring attraction. The Friends organise a number of events each year, starting with a spring talk, when expert speakers are invited to lecture on subjects such as gardens, horticulture and others fields relevant to the park, its trees, wildlife and plants. (See www.cannizaropark.com for more information).

Herb Garden

1 Morden Hall Park	**10** South Park
2 Potting Shed Café	**11** Surrey Arms Pub
3 Garden Centre	**12** Adventure Play Area
4 Stable Yard	**13** White Bridge
5 Snuff Mill	**14** Morden Hall
6 River Wandle	**15** Wetlands
7 Morden Cottage	**16** North Park
8 Rose Garden	**17** Wandle Trail
9 Arboretum	**18** Deen City Farm

● Places of Interest   ● Food & Drink

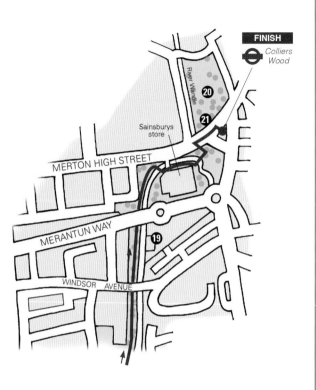

19 Merton Abbey Mills

20 Wandle Park

21 Charles Holden Pub

Morden Hall Park & Wandle Trail

Distance: 3mi (4.8km)

Terrain: easy, relatively flat

Duration: 1½ hours

Open: unrestricted access to park

Start: Morden tube

End: Colliers Wood tube

Postcode: SM4 5JD

A tranquil former deer park, Morden Hall Park is one of the few estates to survive from those that lined the River Wandle during its industrial heyday. It was home to the Garth family from the 16th century onwards, although the current house dates from the mid-18th century. In 1873 the estate was purchased by tobacco merchant Gilliat Hatfeild, who created much of the current park. His son Gilliat Edward Hatfeild (1864-1941), a bachelor, left the estate to the National Trust on his death. Today, it covers 125 acres (50ha), encompassing Morden Hall, its stable yard, pretty Morden Cottage, and many old farm buildings.

Sited on the flood plain of the Wandle, the estate features three main habitats: meadow, marsh and woodland. Water lies at the heart of Morden Hall, and the lush wetlands, riverbanks and islands provide an ideal habitat for a variety of plants, mammals (such as voles and pipistrelle bats), insects and birdlife. Cormorants, kingfishers, ducks and swans are regularly seen along the river, and there's a heron colony in the wetlands, which is also visited by a little egret. Rarer birds such as warblers, redwings and firecrests shelter in the hedgerows, while woodpeckers and owls live in the woods.

The meadows are managed to provide a mixture of natural grasses and wildflowers during summer, while the marshes and river's edge offer wetland habitats for flowers such as yellow iris and marsh marigold. There's also an ornamental avenue of lime and horse chestnut trees, and a mulberry tree thought to have been planted by Huguenots in the 18th century. The park has other native trees such as oak, beech, ash, birch, and some lovely riverside willows and alders, plus one of England's oldest yews.

Morden Hall Park & Wandle Trail

The Wandle is a typical chalk stream, rising from a spring near South Croydon and running 12½ miles (20km) to its mouth at Wandsworth on the River Thames. The fast-flowing river has been employed by people living along its banks since prehistoric times, first as a source of water and fish, and later for power to drive waterwheels. In its heyday in the 18th and 19th centuries there were around 50 working mills on the Wandle, when it was the most industrialised river in the world.

Morden Hall Park sits in the middle of the Wandle Trail (a hiking and cycling path), which follows the course of the river, and our walk takes you on a tour of the park and follows a section of the trail, via historic Merton Abbey Mills, to Colliers Wood.

Start Walking…

Exit from Morden tube station, cross London Road and walk along Aberconway Road (there's a Lidl on the right). At the end of the road cross Morden Hall Road

---

Stable Yard

Constructed around 1879 to house carriage and riding horses, the Stable Yard gives an indication of the Hatfeilds' wealth. Note the trout on the weather vane, reflecting the links with the River Wandle and fishing.

---

at the traffic lights and turn right, and a bit further along on the left is the entrance to **Morden Hall Park ❶** (unrestricted access) via green double gates; the free car park is 100m further along on the left. Through the gates, follow the path with the water channel on your left, part of a river-fed moat around Morden Hall. On your right is the **Potting Shed Café 2** – a good choice for morning coffee or lunch – and the **Garden Centre ❸** (both open 9am-5/6pm), the National Trust's first such venture. There are free guided tours of the park on Sundays at 11.30am and 1pm starting from here.

Continue straight ahead past a group of buildings that were part of the former estate, including a boiler house, various sheds and stables (originally for working ponies), some of which are now

Morden Hall Park & Wandle River

leased to local craftspeople. A bit further on is the **Stable Yard** ❹ (open 8am-5/6pm, see box) on the left, now an energy-efficient eco building housing a visitor centre, gallery, second-hand bookshop and café. On the right is the former **Snuff Mill** ❺ (see box) which closed in 1922 and is now a Learning Centre providing activities for local groups. The old water mill is still in situ but is no longer in operation (look for the eel pass on the left-hand side of the wheel, which allows eels to navigate the river).

A path leads past the Snuff Mill and across the bridge over the **River Wandle** ❻, with picturesque **Morden Cottage** ❼ on the right. The cottage is now part of the London Acorn School, a holistic school for children aged 3 to 14, where pupils are

> ### Snuff Mill
>
> The Hatfeild fortune came from drying and grinding tobacco into a fine powder known as snuff. The original waterwheel, now restored, powered the huge millstones to crush the tobacco. The millstones on display are actually from a spice mill, but are typical of the stones used. Behind the old watermill is its modern equivalent, an Archimedes screw hydro-electric turbine, which generates electricity for the park's visitor centre.

some 2,000 roses including 25 varieties of floribunda roses displayed across 38 beds, and is at its fragrant best between mid-June and mid-July, but is often still in flower in early autumn. There's a historical link between roses and the snuff industry, which financed the estate for so many years, as roses are used to scent snuff, although they weren't used for that purpose here. The garden hosts an outdoor theatre in summer.

Follow the path past the rose garden and go through the iron gates, turn right over the tarmac bridge across a stream and immediately right again along the narrow path that runs alongside the stream and the railings of the rose garden. This area is the **Arboretum** ❾, containing an unusual collection of ornamental trees, including a ginkgo biloba and hornbeam (in the rose garden) and one of the oldest

Arboretum

banned from using smartphones, computers and watching TV – even at home! Just past the school is the beautiful 2½-acre **Rose Garden** ❽, planted around 1921 by Gilliat Edward Hatfeild, who lived in Morden Cottage in preference to the Hall. It contains

White Bridge & Morden Hall

yews in England. Continue along the path, which meanders along the course of the Wandle into **South Park** ❿ . In the 18th century this was a deer park, although by the mid-20th century cattle had gradually replaced the deer. Today, it's a lovely area of wildflower meadows and a favourite picnic spot.

There are restored 18th-century statues of Neptune and Venus on an island in the River Wandle alongside the path, where gunnera or giant rhubarb can be seen in summer. Keep to the left where the path forks at a pond and you soon come to an avenue of lime and horse chestnut trees – a riot of colour in the autumn – near the gate by the **Surrey Arms** ⓫ pub; in the 18th and 19th centuries, avenues of lime trees were a status symbol, while horse chestnuts were also fashionable. Continue on the path around the perimeter of the park past a Tramlink (Phipps Bridge)

Morden Hall

Built between 1750 and 1765 within a moated enclosure created from the Wandle, the hall was home to the Garth family for generations, and later to tobacco merchant Gilliat Hatfeild. During World War One, it was a military hospital and has been a restaurant in recent times. It's now a wedding venue.

---

tram stop – look out for a bright yellow Acer cappadocicum on the left as you approach the stop – where the path veers left towards Morden Hall. After around 300m cross back over the tarmac bridge (which you crossed earlier) and continue straight ahead.

In the trees on the right – opposite the entrance to the park – there's an **Adventure Play Area** ⓬ for children, equipped with swings, a play fort, climbing posts and a zipwire. Around 100m further on, cross over the iconic Victorian wrought iron **White Bridge** ⓭ over the Wandle – a favourite spot for playing pooh sticks and for wedding photos – beyond which is a second white bridge (closed) leading to **Morden Hall** ⓮ beyond. There are rare swamp cypresses and a deciduous conifer on the White Bridge lawn.

From the White Bridge turn right and follow the path as it crosses over two small wooden bridges. There are two parallel branches of the Wandle here, which join into one just before Deen City

Farm (see below). Turn right after the second bridge and follow the (dragonfly) signpost to the lush **Wetlands** ⑮, a flooded area that's home to a rich variety of wildlife, including one of the closest heronries to central London. After around 200m the path changes to a recently created boardwalk, which zigzags its way left across the wetlands. On a platform in the middle of the boardwalk there are benches and an elevated viewing platform, where notices provide information on what you might see – a kingfisher, egret or heron if you're lucky.

Just after the end of the boardwalk the path to the right leads to the tramline (where you head later) but for now go straight ahead to **North Park** ⑯ and follow the path to the end and down the other side, where you take the first path on the left to the tram crossing (with the wetlands on your right). Continue to the end of the path and cross the tramline via the wooden bridge (take care when crossing!). Follow the path

Food & Drink

② **Potting Shed Café:** The National Trust café occupies a riverside setting at the entrance to Merton Hall Park, serving homemade lunches and cakes (9am-5/6pm, £).

⑲ **Merton Abbey Mills:** The former mill buildings contain a number of restaurants, cafés and pubs (10am-5pm, closed Mon-Tue, £).

㉑ **The Charles Holden:** A traditional pub offering good ales and food (Sunday roast) and a large beer garden (noon-11pm/midnight, £)

round to the right – past a large warehouse – where it continues along the River Wandle and the **Wandle Trail** ⑰.

After around 400m you come to **Deen City Farm** ⑱ (10am-4.30pm, closed Mondays), which has a café, farm shop, small animal enclosures and a riding school. Continue along the driveway past the farm (with the river on your right) and cross

Wetlands boardwalk

over Windsor Avenue. From here, you're back on a footpath and around 100m further on you pass the Pickle Ditch on the right (the old course of the River Wandle). A short distance past the ditch cross a bridge on your right to **Merton Abbey Mills** 19 (see box), which houses restaurants, cafés, bars, boutique shops, arts and crafts, a theatre and a weekend market.

Leaving Merton Abbey Mills, follow the path through the buildings and cross back over the Wandle, and turn right to continue along the Wandle Trail. The path leads under Merantun Way and over Station Road, where it continues along the river. Here, the Wandle follows a wide arc before running parallel to Merton High Street. Just before you reach the High Street, turn right over a footbridge to cross the river, then left along the riverside path where there's a large Sainsbury's on the right. A little further on cross the Pickle Ditch – as it rejoins the current course of the Wandle – via a footbridge and follow the path around the Kiss Me Hardy warehouse to Merton High Street, with **Wandle Park** 20 opposite. Colliers Wood tube station – and the end of this walk – is 200m further along on the right.

The Wandle Trail continues north through Wandle Park for another 4 miles (6.4km) to Wandsworth and the River Thames. If you feel like a drink or something to eat after your exertions, the **Charles Holden** 21 pub opposite, just before the tube station, is a good choice.

Merton Abbey Mills

The mills take their name from Merton Priory, an important Augustinian monastery built in the early 12th century. The idyllic riverside setting was acquired by William Morris in 1881 and was also the site of the Arthur Liberty silk printing works from 1904 until the 1970s. Today, the waterwheel (1885) is the only fully working Victorian wheel in the country, and the only one driven by water power. Nowadays the wheelhouse is a pottery workshop and gallery (the waterwheel is used to turn the potter's wheel). The site's oldest building dates back over 400 years – part of which may be from the priory – and is now the Colour House Theatre.

The Best of London: Capital of Cool

ISBN: 978-1-909282-92-6, 256 pages, £11.99, David Hampshire

There are great world cities, from classical capitals to modern metropolises, and then there's London – the yardstick by which other cities are measured. It has the most astonishing ability to reinvent itself, always staying one step ahead of the pack, a magnet for creatives – be they writers or artists, designers or thinkers – and a melting pot of cultures from around the globe. New York may be hip, Paris may be chic, but London is surely the Capital of Cool.

London for Foodies, Gourmets & Gluttons

ISBN: 978-1-909282-76-6, 288 pages £11.95, David Hampshire & Graeme Chesters

London for Foodies, Gourmets & Gluttons is much more than simply a directory of cafés, markets, restaurants and food shops. It features many of the city's best artisan producers and purveyors, plus a wealth of classes where you can learn how to prepare and cook food like the experts, appreciate fine wines and brew coffee like a barista. And when you're too tired to cook or just want to treat yourself, we'll show you great places where you

can enjoy everything from tea and cake to a tasty street snack; a pie and a pint to a glass of wine and tapas; and a quick working lunch to a full-blown gastronomic extravaganza.

London's Best Shops & Markets

ISBN: 978-1-909282-81-0, 256 pages £12.95, David Hampshire

The UK is a nation of diehard shoppers. Retail therapy is the country's favourite leisure activity – an all-consuming passion – and London is its beating heart. It's one of the world's most exciting shopping cities, packed with grand department stores, trend-setting boutiques, timeless traditional traders, edgy concept stores, absorbing antiques centres, eccentric novelty shops, exclusive purveyors of luxury goods, mouth-watering food emporiums, bustling markets and much more.

see www.survivalbooks.net

INDEX

T

V

W

XY

London's Secrets

LONDON'S HIDDEN SECRETS

ISBN: 978-1-907339-40-0

£10.95, 320 pages, colour

Graeme Chesters

A unique and unusual guide to London's hidden and lesser-known sights not found in standard guidebooks. London is a city with a cornucopia of secret places, being ancient, vast and in a constant state of flux.

London's Hidden Secrets takes you off the beaten path to seek out the more unusual places that often fail to register on the radar of both visitors and residents alike, and aims to sidestep the chaos and queues of London's tourist-clogged attractions and visit its quirkier, more mysterious side.

LONDON'S SECRETS: BIZARRE & CURIOUS

ISBN: 978-1-909282-58-2

£11.95, 320 pages, colour

Graeme Chesters

London is a city with 2,000 years of history, over which it has accumulated a wealth of odd and strange buildings, monuments, statues, street trivia and museum exhibits, to name just a few examples.

This book seeks out the city's most bizarre and curious sights and tells the often fascinating story behind them, from the Highgate vampire to the arrest of a dead man, a legal brothel and a former Texas embassy to Roman bikini bottoms and poetic manhole covers, from London's hanging gardens to a restaurant where you dine in the dark.

LONDON'S SECRET PLACES

ISBN: 978-1-907339-92-9

£10.95, 320 pages, colour

Graeme Chesters & David Hampshire

London is one of the world's leading tourist destinations with a wealth of world-class attractions: amazing museums and galleries, beautiful parks and gardens, stunning palaces and grand houses, and much, much more. These are covered in a plethora of excellent tourist guides and online, and need no introduction here.

Not so well known are London's numerous smaller attractions, most of which are neglected by the throngs who descend upon the tourist-clogged major sights. What London's Secret Places does is seek out the city's lesser-known, but no less worthy, 'hidden' attractions.

see www.londons-secrets.com

LONDON'S SECRETS: MUSEUMS & GALLERIES

ISBN: 978-1-907339-96-7

£10.95, 320 pages, colour

Robbi Atilgan & David Hampshire

London is a treasure trove for museum fans and art lovers and one of the world's great art and cultural centres, with more popular museums and galleries than any other world city. The art scene is a lot like the city itself – diverse, vast, vibrant and in a constant state of flux – a cornucopia of traditional and cutting-edge, majestic and mundane, world-class and run-of-the-mill, bizarre and brilliant.

So, whether you're an art lover, culture vulture, history buff or just looking for something to entertain the family during the school holidays, you're bound to find inspiration in London. All you need is a comfortable pair of shoes, an open mind – and this book!

LONDON'S SECRETS: PUBS & BARS

ISBN: 978-1-907339-93-6

£10.95, 320 pages, colour

Graeme Chesters

British pubs and bars are world famous for their bonhomie, great atmosphere, good food and fine ales. Nowhere is this more so than in London, which has a plethora of watering holes of all shapes and sizes: classic historic boozers and trendy style bars; traditional riverside inns and luxurious cocktail bars; enticing wine bars and brew pubs; mouth-watering gastro pubs and brasseries; welcoming gay bars and raucous music venues. This book features over 250 of the best.

LONDON'S SECRETS: PARKS & GARDENS

ISBN: 978-1-907339-95-0

£10.95, 320 pages, colour

Robbi Atilgan & David Hampshire

London is one of the world's greenest capital cities, with a wealth of places where you can relax and recharge your batteries. Britain is renowned for its parks and gardens, and nowhere has such beautiful and varied green spaces as London: magnificent royal parks, historic garden cemeteries, majestic ancient forests and woodlands, breathtaking formal country parks, expansive commons, charming small gardens, beautiful garden squares and enchanting 'secret' gardens.

Not all are secrets, of course, but many of London's most beguiling green spaces are known only to insiders and locals.

see www.londons-secrets.com

London's Best-Kept Secrets

ISBN: 978-1-909282-74-2, 320 pages
£10.95, David Hampshire

London Best-Kept Secrets brings together our favourite places – the 'greatest hits' – from our London's Secrets series of books. We take you off the beaten tourist path to seek out the more unusual ('hidden') places that often fail to register on the radar of both visitors and residents alike. Nimbly sidestepping the chaos and queues of London's tourist-clogged attractions, we visit its quirkier, lesser-known, but no less fascinating, side. *London Best-Kept Secrets* takes in some of the city's loveliest hidden gardens and parks, absorbing and poignant museums, great art and architecture, beautiful ancient buildings, magnificent Victorian cemeteries, historic pubs, fascinating markets and much more.

London's Hidden Corners, Lanes & Squares

ISBN: 978-1-909282-69-8, 192 pages
£9.95, Graeme Chesters

The inspiration for this book was the advice of writer and lexicographer Dr Samuel Johnson (1709-1784), who was something of an expert on London, to his friend and biographer James Boswell on the occasion of his trip to London in the 18th century, to 'survey its innumerable little lane and courts'. In the 21st century these are less numerous than in Dr Johnson's time, so we've expanded his brief to include alleys, squares and yards, along with a number of mews, roads, streets and gardens.

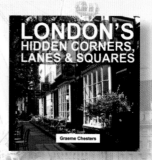

London's Cafés, Coffee Shops & Tearooms

ISBN: 978-1-909282-80-3, 192 pages
£9.95, David Hampshire

This book is a celebration of London's flourishing independent cafés, coffee shops and tearooms – plus places serving afternoon tea and breakfast/brunch – all of which have enjoyed a renaissance in the last decade and done much to strengthen the city's position as one of the world's leading foodie destinations. With a copy of *London's Cafés, Coffee Shops & Tearooms* you'll never be lost for somewhere to enjoy a great cup of coffee or tea and some delicious food.

see www.londons-secrets.com